TRIPOLI THE MYSTERIOUS

This enthralling though tragic coast of northern Africa

TRIPOLI
THE MYSTERIOUS

BY

MABEL LOOMIS TODD
(Mrs. David Todd)

Author of "Total Eclipses of the Sun," "Corona and Coronet," "A Cycle of Sunsets," etc.

Published by Dar Al Fergiani
P.O. Box 132
Tripoli - S.P.L.A.J

First published 1912
This edition 1994

ISBN   1 85077 920 1

Printed in Egypt
By SIJIL AL-ARAB PRESS — Tel.: 932706 Cairo

FOREWORD

The " skirmishes in Tripoli " alluded to casually by newspapers in late September of 1911 soon developed into full-fledged war of international significance.

To an English friend resident there, the first intimation of trouble came in the early morning of September 26, when, from his summer residence at Shara Shat, he and his family saw unexpectedly arrive in the harbour a two-funneled steamer (*Derna*), laden with arms and ammunition which she began at once to discharge.

Next day his little daughter, attending an Italian school in the city, heard a sudden commotion with much loud talking, in the midst of which the Italian *cavasse* and one of the Consulate staff came into the school-room, counseling immediate departure of mistresses and children, most of whom embarked at once on the *Hercules*.

During the latter part of that afternoon a three-funneled battleship arrived, her stately approach watched with much excitement by

FOREWORD

all the inhabitants; Turkish officers and Arabs,
however, expressing the utmost confidence that
the Italian reception would be both warm and
brief.

The *Hercules*, filled from stem to stern with
Italian subjects, sailed next day; and, late on
September 28, thirteen battleships came into
the harbour, one after the other, in stately line,
each proudly flying the Italian flag, and all
brought into spectacular relief by brilliant
African sunshine lighting the magnificent array
with its level westering beams. The sight
created a profound impression, not only upon
native and Turkish inhabitants, but upon the
few remaining Europeans as well.

Next day the Turkish soldiers retired to
Boumilliana; during the following, a sort of
panic ensued among the Maltese, who rushed
en masse on board the *Castlegarth*, — loading
esparto in the roadstead, — and thenceforth
disappeared from the scene. On October 1
Italians cut the cable, about three miles from
shore.

Naturally these swift events produced the
greatest excitement; consular meetings were
held night and day at all hours, advising and
counseling the Governor-General, and Arif

FOREWORD

Bey, political agent; but long parleying finally
exhausted the Italian Admiral's patience, and
October 3 notice was given to all Consuls that
bombardment would take place at noon. Many
trying even then to flee found that Arab boat-
men had drawn their craft up on shore, and
refused to take any one off to any steamer.

The wife of our friend, who kept an interesting diary of these thrilling events, writes
that thereupon "a panic ensued, people rushing about the streets as though they had lost
their senses." Many sought refuge in their
house, — Netherlands subjects, Arabs, Turks,
Greeks, indiscriminately, until courtyard, gallery and rooms could hold no more.

When bombardment finally began the noise
was terrific, houses shaking as if in earthquake,
refugees crying with grief and terror. Our
English friends, however, were not daunted,
and going to the Telegraph Company's house
on the water front, they obtained from its balcony a superb view, remaining until a shell
dropped into the sea about twenty yards away,
shrapnel began to burst all around and break
over them, and it seemed prudent to retreat
to the kiosk on their own roof terrace, —
slightly more protected, but still offering a

FOREWORD

splendid prospect. At six o'clock firing ceased, when, gathering up the bits of fallen shrapnel (not less than twenty pounds), they retired to their populous rooms below.

The following day fire was opened upon Shara Shat with an awful roar of shells traveling through the air, followed by the terrific vibration of their bursting. A mistake of the Shara Shat fort in firing upon a torpedo boat supposedly flying a white flag was the immediate cause of this second fusillade, which ceased upon explanation — but not until the country house was partially demolished. In the following weeks it was completely looted and left open to all the winds of heaven.

During this day the *gens d'armes* and police who had been on guard were withdrawn, and there was much apprehension that the city would be overwhelmed by the onrushing Arabs. Hassuna Pasha, the Mayor, a Prince of the famous Caramanlis, however, himself patrolled the town all night on horseback, with a few police, keeping at bay the oncoming hordes. Rifle shots and shouts kept sleep from every house.

On October 5 a white sheet was hoisted on the Castle flagstaff, the Italians landed, and soon it was replaced by a large flag of their country. Safety returned to the harassed inhabitants, and the city was soon being regularly patrolled by marines.

Later, when Italians blew up the Gil Gursh fort, the city shook to its foundations and our friend's fine collection of Roman antiquities was strewn in fragments on the floor. By the end of October cholera had broken out, which added new terror and confusion. Mosques were filled with poor Arabs from the oasis, ordered evacuated by General Caneva, the Governor. Dead bodies were picked up by carts at morning and evening and carried away for burial.

A heavy fight occurred November 10, a day also memorable for the appearance of a great yellow balloon carrying two Italian officers making observations. Next day the Italian King's birthday was celebrated by salutes, "dressed" ship, a shell or two whizzing through the air, and an official reception.

The new year saw more battles, and a vast change in the sleepy Tripoli of our memory. Italian soldiers now fill the streets; horses, carriages, motor cars (with no speed limit!), officers on horseback, and all the accompaniments

FOREWORD

of modern seaport life have completely changed the old dream-city, now forever of the past.

No more at twilight are Arabs sitting in the sand against mosque walls like a line of ghosts in the still evening, waiting for the call to prayer. The " gate of slaves," one of Tripoli's ancient names, will never more open its portals for that picturesque if ungodly trade; dwellers in Ghadames, making business to the heart of Ethiopia all their own, and allied with the fanatical Tuaregs, those unconquerable " pirates of the Sahara," will have new laws to consider.

But in dreaming upon the delicious, sleepy days of past years, the cordial faces of many friends beam from the white city's every archway and *patio,* smile upon us from roof and garden — even from dusky mosque and heaven-ascending minaret.

To them all, loved and remembered, English, Turkish, Italian, French, Arab — I dedicate my little story of the now vanished life we knew together, affectionately theirs as well as mine.

M. L. T.

Observatory House,
Amherst, Massachusetts,
March, 1912.

TABLE OF CONTENTS

TABLE OF CONTENTS

ILLUSTRATIONS

                        xiii

ILLUSTRATIONS

ILLUSTRATIONS

TRIPOLI THE MYSTERIOUS

I

INTRODUCTORY

Properly to write the wonderful story of Tripoli, daughter of sea and desert, one must be not only an accomplished historian, a cultivated archæologist and an expert in ethnology, but profoundly versed in Arabic and in the fundamental beliefs and general practices of Mohammedanism, as well as the local customs of that great religion, coloured as it is by differing environment. If one aims to give a clear exposition of this enthralling though tragic coast of northern Africa, he must be a thorough student of political economy, too, with a world outlook on cause and effect in government.

Tripoli of the West enjoys the protection of a natural rocky breakwater, obvious proof

that a city has always been there, ever since
the earliest voyages of Phœnician navigators.
Conquered by Rome, and held in splendid prosperity until the seventh century of our era,
inundated by Moslems, prey of Vandals, captured by Charles V, ruled by native Pashas,
seized by Turkey, bombarded by Italy — who
has the ethical right to Tripoli to-day?

The exciting events of 1911 have directed
more popular attention to Tripoli than she had
enjoyed for over a century. She will never
be wholly forgotten again. Why the fascinating oriental city had been so ignored is
difficult to see; but repeated visits there for
astronomical purposes had revealed a charm
of living and a wealth of history that years
of study and observation could not exhaust.

Among the most scholarly men in Tripoli
were certain Jewish rabbis whose minds were
storehouses of information. As they spoke
only Hebrew I conversed with them through
interpreters, but a rich field of investigation
here awaits translation to the general student.

2

INTRODUCTORY

If we of the English-writing world are able to speak French and German fairly well, we feel more or less equipped for cosmopolitan living; with a smattering of Spanish and Italian in addition we are thought unusual linguists, quite competent to conquer the world. But what of the other well-nigh countless tongues of millions.

Even the small boys of Tripoli's narrow streets can use interchangeably all the languages current there. Americans would be quite at sea in that whirlwind of dialect.

A daughter of the Consul-General of Great Britain illustrated the true cosmopolitan, at home in the world at large: many an afternoon have I seen her dispensing tea to half a dozen nationalities, addressing each in his own language, turning instantly and gracefully from one to another with English, French, Turkish, Italian, Arabic, modern Greek, Maltese — on the tip of her clever and fluent tongue.

Only by such versatility and flexibility of

3

make-up can one cope with the endless and complicated problems of such a racial composite.

In view of the far-reaching nature of Tripoli and her story, I will only add that this book does not even touch upon a thousand and one delightful aspects of the white city which might be brought out. In spite of months of residence there and constant eagerness for all its enchanting phases, I bring only an incomplete picture of the extraordinary region as I saw it, though drawn with a loving and appreciative hand.

Italian pharmacy

II

Tripoli the Mysterious

With her feet in the blue Mediterranean, "her head in the fire of heaven" and her back against the yellow silence of eternal Sahara, Tripoli waits her latest destiny.

However diplomatic complications may be solved, lethargic, oriental, half-mediæval Tripoli will be no more. The old walled city of Roman, Arab and Turk must awake at last and take her place in the procession of the modern world.

For years hinted foreboding and prophecies of change were quietly pervasive. While much of its trade was in the hands of Jews and Maltese, Italy, having other large interests in the region, had practically absorbed the shipping. " Sometime Tripoli will be Italian " was whispered in many tongues.

5

TRIPOLI THE MYSTERIOUS

Compulsory service in the Turkish army was not wholly to the liking of independent native tribes, and despite faith in one prophet, a sort of watchful neutrality characterized the Arabs, perhaps even more marked than in usual relations of the conquered to their " protectors." At all events a certain restlessness was obvious among Maltese, Italians, even in calmer sons of the desert, and no one who knew Tripoli city could have been surprised at the seemingly sudden *coup d'état* of her nearest European neighbor.

One of the last regions in this over-traveled world not only unswamped, but even unnoticed by tourists, the old Tripoli of Punic and Roman days and of later Mohammedan supremacy can never again retreat into the obscurity of centuries.

It has been said that Tripoli stands as a sort of buffer between Tunis and Egypt. Both France and England would seem to have looked indifferently upon her unproductive wastes; but the position of Italy, alive to her

Compulsory service in the Turkish army

value, is somewhat different, and in the eyes of many careful observers it has been considered the European power most likely sometime to conquer and govern the desert province. Rome once reigned supreme over northern Africa. Why not claim again a part of her early heritage? Natural outlet for the wealth of Africa, Tripoli might be made a place of especial importance in judicious hands.

The battles of 1911 seem almost contradictory when we consider that Mohammedans are fatalists: all Arabs say " Fate is irrevocable, and to oppose destiny is sacrilege." Perhaps, however, the Tripolitan mind was not wholly certain as to just what constituted its decreed destiny.

More picturesque under Ottoman rule than it can ever be again, — dreamy, dirty, sordid, exquisite, noisy, enthralling, beautiful, unsanitary, — the strange city gripped one's affections. Into the heart it came to stay.

III

An Eclipse Trip to Tripoli

Twice the alliterative delight of "an eclipse trip to Tripoli" has been ours. In May of 1900 the sun's anticipated darkening brought us to those dazzling shores; and again in August, 1905, by a coincidence unique in astronomical annals, another eclipse track crossed the former one exactly over the same populous city. Knowing its limpid skies and freedom from cloud, the Astronomer and his retinue once more set forth for this far shore.

If "science acquaints us with strange bedfellows," eclipse paths are responsible for enticing their followers into remote and untraveled ways which are extremely likely to prove mines of heretofore unsuspected wealth, in landscape, ethnology, picturesque history and customs, and all the charm of unspoiled humanity.

8

AN ECLIPSE TRIP TO TRIPOLI

This was emphatically true of Tripoli, Tra-blus el-Gharb (Tripoli of the West), that famous Oea of the ancients, whose long and troubled history began in the mists of Phœnician founding, ran through the splendid period of Roman rule, saw all its previous glory wiped out and rendered naught after the Hejira in A. D. 622, when Islam overran the whole North African coast like an irresistible tidal wave, and in 1835 reduced it to the fate of a Turkish vilayet. All the charm of all these varied fates hung about its narrow streets, impassive white walls, arcaded thoroughfares, headless statues and whitewashed tiles, its bubbling domes and sky-piercing minarets.

The advent of an astronomer and his apparatus had excited more intense interest than Arab imperturbability would allow to become apparent. That he had come across far seas for an eclipse, whatever that might be, was an event of amazing import.

During my frequent visits to harems I heard much speculation, curiosity, and not a

9

little fear expressed, as to some event approaching both strange and portentous. An
old man near the sea-gate gave out that he
retained a memory of such an occurrence
years before. But that darkening was made
by Allah. Of this new kind, produced by a
kafir, he could know nothing, nor ought it to
be countenanced. Others scouted the idea that
a kafir could accomplish it.

While Arabs were among the first to tell the
world of astronomy, this science seems practically unknown to the inhabitants of Barbary,
who cannot calculate eclipses, and believe they
always bring or foretell evil. In some quarters of the city it was asserted that enormous
balloons had been brought as essential parts
of the outfit, and that when the appointed day
should come, the Astronomer would ascend
straight into the " eye of the sun," there to
discharge five hundred pounds' worth (ster-
ling) of spirits of wine, which in evaporating
would cause thick darkness and eclipse. Some
of the more intelligent having been asked to

draw the corona, replied that it was forbidden to gaze upon such a thing, much less attempt to depict it, and would be followed by certain disaster.

On our second visit, wonder and suspicion had changed to friendliness, and no evil was prophesied from our manipulation of the heavens.

As before, by courtesy of H.M. representative, the Astronomer had established his observing station on the roof-terrace of the British Consulate-General, soon again popularly known as the " royal observatory," where telescopic groves grew apace, to the wonderment of upward-gazing multitudes from lower roofs.

But the whole region was pregnant with absorbing interest, quite detached from astronomy; and while my husband was constantly engaged with his apparatus and eclipse preparation, in the intervals of such minor aid as I might render in the preparations, I found every moment occupied.

TRIPOLI THE MYSTERIOUS

With the blue sea, sands and city dazzling white, Arabs and Bedouins baffling and mysterious, relics steeped in half-forgotten history, every fallen stone full of suggestion, near neighbour to countless sand-blown ruins, each with its dumb story awaiting interpretation, Tripoli offered unimagined material to artist, archæologist and historian, as well as to delvers into racial problems, and linguistic students of many dialects.

To revisit any spot once loved and deserted has been called by Lafcadio Hearn a dangerous experiment. But our return to these fair shores did not disenchant. Potent even in absence, the fascination only increased as the sight of her sunny whiteness grew again into actual vision, and became one with memory.

And now again the story of Tripoli changes. But whatever the outcome, she will have still her limpid skies, her air like wine, and a climate where it is a sin to acknowledge an ache or a pain, old age or unhappiness. The charm of Orient and Islam may be less; but I can

Near neighbor to countless sand-blown ruins

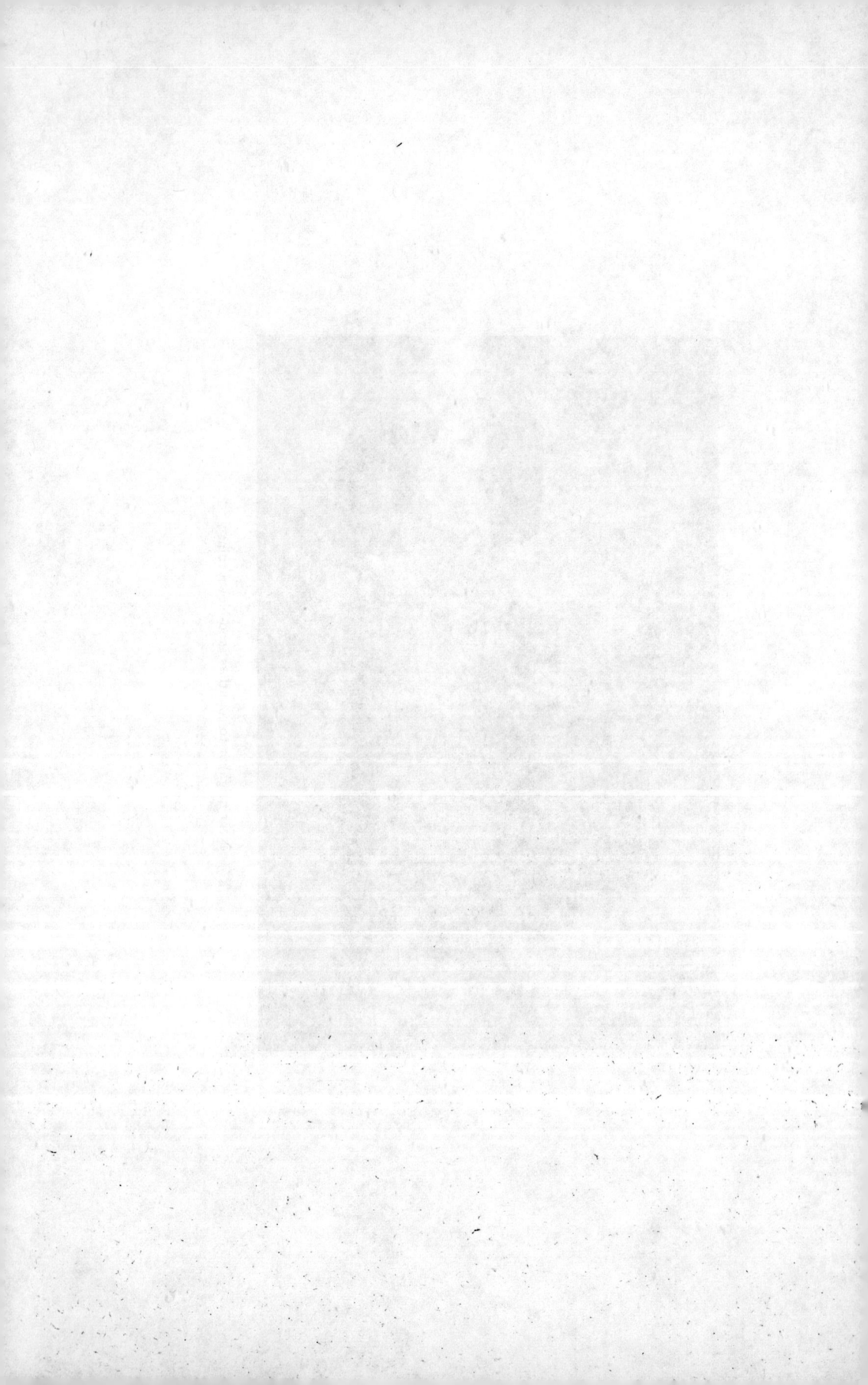

AN ECLIPSE TRIP TO TRIPOLI

never cease to be grateful that I knew Tripoli
in the days when to breathe her atmosphere
and revel in her sunshine meant joy, not
only, but when crowding nationalities, Babel
tongues, mediæval streets, brought such vivify-
ing interest that all the years thereafter have
been richer, more satisfying, and fuller of the
intoxicating wine of life.

IV

ARRIVAL

In childhood we all learned the " four Barbary States, — Morocco, Algeria, Tunis and
Tripoli." Perhaps in after years some of the
little pupils who recited that list so glibly may
have seen Morocco or Algiers, perhaps even
Tunis; but it is safe to say that few ever
saw Tripoli, to other lands a name only for
many generations.

The province of Tripoli contains practically
everything for eight hundred miles between
Djerba and Tobrook, from Tunis to Egypt,
and southward to Fezzan, the town of Ghadames and the oasis of Ghat. The island of
Djerba was the scene of terrible conflict between Moors and Spaniards during the Sara-
cenic wars of the Middle Ages. There are
traces upon the north coast of a pyramid built

14

of the skulls of Christians, as a warning not to attempt another subjugation of the island.

Methods of reaching Tripoli are leisurely. From Naples a line of comfortable Italian steamers runs to Messina, and down the beautiful coast of Sicily, with unhurried stops at Catania and Syracuse, thence across to Malta, where one has hours for Valetta and its suburbs. Early morning arrival in the sparkling harbour of Tripoli was an almost theatrical vision of strange craft flying Greek, Turkish, Italian, French flags, and small native boats, fishermen, sponge-divers and all the curious life of a peculiarly non-European community.

Another route to the same bourne is by French steamer from Marseilles to Tunis. Full of interest in itself, this French-Arab city, glowing and enticing on the far shores of its salt lagoon, is actually less vital with all its abounding life than the near-by site of ancient Carthage alive with memory. Over the wrecked beauty and splendour buried in the yellow earth, a gleaming little Arab village

lies asleep in the sun, prone upon the hillside.
From Carthage eastward along the curving
coast-line, the steamer stops at Mehdia, Sousse,
Sfax, Gabes, full of superb relics; dim African mountains brood, a swarming Moslem life
fills pier and promontory, until all is crowned
at last by the white flash of Tripoli, dazzling
in hot sunshine — the ideal Africa of one's
imagination.

Many Arabian authors have described this
ancient city from the sea with all the wealth
of fancy and richness of imagery they knew
so well. But the beauty of that spectacle
could not have been exaggerated.

The old wall, the Pasha's Castle, the exquisite rounded mosques, many a minaret holding aloft its golden pinnacles and crescent,
feathery palms, a green band separating sea
from sand dunes and desert, and two lovely
domed tombs standing alone on a little point,
all made a vision of ethereal loveliness. The
ancient lighthouse seemed not an extraneous
structure, but an integral part of the tide-

washed rocks from which it grew; and beyond, in the city, flags of many countries seemed keeping perpetual holiday. Above the official residence of the British Consul-General the national emblem waved silent welcome, only next in affection to the stars and stripes which nowhere appeared. Oriental, mediæval, picturesque, unthought of by the traveler, unvisited by the tourist, Tripoli seemed left behind in the breathless rush of modern life.

The whole impression of a first arrival soon became separated into component parts. Greek sponge boats, hauled up high and dry on the beach for repairs, the sea-gate (Bab el-Bahr) open for the day, Turkish officials idling and smoking on benches, Greek sailors pulling at narghiles, Arabs taking cups of black coffee in a dozen corners — sharp contrasts filled this strange, fascinating city of the prophet.

V

THOROUGHFARES

One's first walk is a revelation of oriental possibilities.

"Balik! Balik!" One jumps aside at the sudden, harsh cry; and a tiny, overloaded donkey trots by patiently, its little hoofs soundless on the white and powdery street. Generally weighed down with grass panniers holding huge earthern-ware water-jars, often the carcass of a sheep or lamb, and perhaps his owner in addition (sitting, however, mercifully well back upon the little animal's haunches, unless he is walking behind, the better to goad the hurrying flanks), countless numbers of the pathetic little beasts trot eagerly along, helpless ears wagging to and fro, always humble, always sad, with woes which never rise to the dignity of genuine sorrows.

But no warning shout gives notice of the

One's first walk is a revelation of Oriental possibilities

camel's stealthy approach. His padded feet move on like fate. No other traveler has any rights which he is bound to respect, and a scornful face with indescribably contemptuous and curling under lip may be thrust over one's very shoulder from the rear, without other notice than his unannounced proximity.

For many reasons, indeed, one must be wary in the narrow streets. It is the pedestrian's own fault if donkeys, goats, camels or the occasional two-wheeled, canopied *araba* run him down. Caution is soon learned. After all, the camel does not seem to feel the same lively enmity to Caucasians so openly evinced by the sinister water buffalo of the Philippines. His lofty hauteur is too great to admit so personal a sensation as dislike.

And he has a variety of voices.

During one of my first nights in the white city, when awakened by a prolonged and screaming cry, I thought sleepily of a locomotive in trouble. A slight accession of consciousness showed the impossibility of hearing

railway sounds through several hundred miles:
it was merely the night call of the domesti-
cated camel, trumpeting his perennial discon-
tent to some fellow sufferer; or perchance
dreaming of free, windblown desert spaces,
no more home for his longing feet. With Kip-
ling we came to feel that —

"'E's a devil an' a' ostrich an' a' orphan child in one."

In the narrow thoroughfares he passes with
infinite disdain; but in one wide-open room,
with its arched ceiling, another camel, blinded
by oval baskets tied over his eyes, used to
tread his monotonous round year after year,
grinding corn between upper and nether mill-
stones. Centuries of habit lay behind the
primitive appliances.

Slightly at one side of the thronging highways, in corners and niches here and there, a
bundle of rags appeared to have been thrown,
carelessly; to one's surprise these huddled
masses once in a while sat up, peacefully adjusted themselves, and stalked away, dignified,

fully dressed Arabs. The barracan, indeed, is apt to be costume by day, bed, pillow and cover by night.

The chorus of street cries was singularly varied. Potatoes, oranges, fish, peculiarly white eggs sold by jet black men, — each article was accompanied by its special tone and tune, language or dialect.

In front of their open shops devout Arabs read the Koran in apparent absorption; never so far removed from this world's affairs, however, as to forget the additional price for their wares reserved for Christians.

Bakers without warning pulled out from their ovens huge shovels full of yellow loaves, until the long iron handles, reaching nearly across the street, proved a sudden stumbling-block to the unwary. This sulphur-tinted edible is more decorative than hygienic. But it must be distinctly convenient to use the street as a sort of supplementary bake-shop, when one's own premises are too small for manipulating the long-handled implements of

trade; and no less easy and pleasant to strew
one's loaves along the highway, where cus-
tomers here and there can pick up those most
to their liking, drop an infinitesimal Turkish
coin, and pass silently onward.

In the street of potters pretty Jewish boys
made and sold jars identical in shape with the
Roman amphoræ of two thousand years ago,
still frequently unearthed when wells were
dug, or a new garden made. Digging for
relics *per se* was forbidden by the Turkish
government; but among those interested in
antiquities many wells seemed an imperative
necessity. The modern copies were still carried off to small inland villages, as they had
been since the dawn of history, over roads
and scarcely discernible pathways of immemo-
rial age, quite as bad as when first trodden.

The city streets were no better; and for
considerations of cleanliness walks were generally taken in the morning. Small boys went
about at sunrise, sweeping with the bushy part
of the date palm, and collecting accumulated

The two-wheeled *araba* was a very gay little cart

rubbish in baskets, took it to the beach for burning. During the day, however, house-keepers gradually threw out into the street augmenting piles of everything discarded — decaying vegetables, fruit, bones, eggshells, fish, all imaginable refuse — so that toward sunset walking, at all times precarious, was but divided pleasure.

The two-wheeled *araba* was a very gay little cart, with bright awnings and blue paint, deco-rated with fancy designs, as well as red cur-tains against the blinding sun. But it had no springs, and the axle lay uncovered on the floor, inconveniences scarcely compensated on unpaved thoroughfares by a string of merrily jingling bells around the horse's neck. Later the use of these conveyances had been forbid-den by the Pasha, who insisted upon fine vic-torias drawn by two horses. Donkeys and camels as means of locomotion had no serious rivals in those early days.

Along the narrow, tunnel-like thorough-fares, all occupations seemed to be going on

23

in the face and eyes of the public. Pale " blue-wash " tinted many of the arches, or pink or yellow, yet hardly affecting the general white-ness of effect. Sometimes the streets were roofed with matting to keep off the scorching sun; or treated, pergola-fashion, with grape-vines hanging their clusters overhead, above the hurrying throngs.

Weaving with the most primitive of looms went on in one street, each occupation having its own quarter where all shops and houses were devoted to a particular industry. Red and yellow cotton plaids made dusky interiors almost gay as old women bent above their tasks, throwing shuttles and pulling threads in unconsciously picturesque attitudes, while barracans grew visibly under their swiftly flying fingers. But far more beautiful were the soft white fabrics of camel's hair, some-times camel's hair and silk together, more rarely silk alone, making a garment of most poetic quality.

Farther on was the arcade of metal-workers,

Pale blue-wash tinted many of the arches

where pliable native gold and silver were
beaten and cut and hammered clumsily into
shape; bracelets of incredible weight and
flexibility, golden sequins hung upon chains
yards in length, odd ornaments for a people
left over from mediæval times, knowing and
using nothing different from those of generations ago. The silent workers glanced up in-
curiously at the passer, and bent once more
to their tasks. With the street throngs it
was quite different; closing in about us in
a tightly wedged crowd, dozens of personal
articles were proffered at double their value.

Over every shop was painted, carved or
otherwise indicated, the hand which averts
the evil eye quite as effectively as unclosing
fingers, extended towards dangerous persons,
and accompanied by the universal "hamsa!
hamsa!"

Round, rectangular or oval leather cushions
were found in another quarter, decorated in
rough patterns, the outlines burned to a deep
brown, the colouring soft reds and yellows with

25

more or less black. Rugs, too, were woven
in similar colours, but small, without pile, and
not always straight or symmetrical; these
could be well seen and studied in the bazars
which contained many products of the region,
where African ethnology became an absorbing
subject.

But in a city devoid of tourists nothing was
arranged with an eye to captivate foreign attention, and one needed to search and inquire
for wares which in more sophisticated Tunis
or Algiers would be alluringly displayed. By
effort, however, dusty shelves and unsuspected
corners could be made to reveal beautiful old
brass lamps, manifestly Grecian and Italian,
candle-sticks, door-knockers, handles, all black
with age and neglect, but graceful and artistic.

A great rallying point in the city was the
Turkish fountain, erected in honour of the
present Sultan's predecessor, and always surrounded by a varied throng at all hours. One
passed it in most of the drives or rides out-

A great rallying-point . . . was the Turkish fountain

side, along the mud-walled lanes leading to the great desert where eternity waits.

A few carvers of ivory were still found here and there, and by giving the design and carefully indicating shapes and uses, fairly good work was obtained. Upon urgent request, parasol handles of ivory with ingeni- ously sliding rings were made, even a mono- gram carved, although the artisan had not the faintest knowledge of the letters or their significance.

One old man continued to make grass and palm fans in shape like a square flag, ordi- narily with carved olive wood handles; but very sumptuous ivory handles could be sub- stituted by giving detailed orders, and one's initials could be neatly woven into the fan itself. A little carving, too, was done by na- tives on ostrich eggs, but better work in this line was shown by Italians. Ostrich feathers from the interior were still exported to some extent, sorting of the dull, brownish plumes as to size, fulness and other qualities being entrusted to Arab and Jewish boys under watchful direction.

In 1900 the city was heavily walled. The small English colony had constructed tennis courts in a convenient angle outside the great barricade, and afternoon tea was served, following the vigourous games every day. At six o'clock, when sunset was beginning to flush all the white masonry with a delicious pink, the ponderous gates were closed to all outsiders, and no one went or came through again until morning.

When the great gates swung together, they met on a brass plate in the street. Whoever in departing from the city should unwittingly step on it was destined to return. That was my happy fortune in 1900 and lo! I once more saw the desert city five years later, but by that time the gates and part of the wall had been removed. Some vague feeling for European boulevard effects had dawned, and a street along the water was laid out with a sea wall and railing. But no paving had been

Some vague feeling for European boulevard effects

attempted, and alternate hill and valley still made progress in any wheeled vehicle an impossible torture.

One lovely May morning I was awakened very early by droves of goats passing, their little hoofs making a chorus of clicks on the road; and apparently they were attached to a cavalcade of bells which rang with continued insistence as if intentionally awakening the city.

Later in the day a street fight occurred between a jet-black vendor of bottles carried about in a little push-cart and a lighter coloured, befezzed person, which gradually collected a crowd of all the nations of the earth, among them a man with a table on his head. It sounded as if they were going to tear each other's eyes out, but Arabic is curiously emphatic, and the voices were hoarse and loud at best; after all, it turned out to be a fairly amiable encounter. In the midst, a procession of children in all varieties of supposed European clothes came by, convoyed by two or three pale and anxious-looking Roman Catholic Sisters. Then appeared a heavily turbaned Turk in a gorgeous red robe; then a brown-vestured Franciscan Brother.

Sponge boats were often anchored at the Marina, where we sometimes took afternoon coffee. Old men weaving coarse baskets sat about in corners, and mountains of water-jars of all conceivable sizes and shapes were piled here and there. In the fish market were brilliant scarlet and bright blue fish. Near by on several occasions I saw a holy dervish with bushy, curly hair and beard, the head quite bare of fez and barracan, a look of strange abstraction in his piercing eyes. Marabouts, holy men, passed now and then, reverently saluted on every hand.

Enormous door keys were carried conspicuously by Arabs around the street. In Morocco and Algiers the same habit has been noted; but there it probably has a different significance, as a belief still exists that the Moors driven from Granada will one day return to the homes of their ancestors; and the huge keys so cherished, sometime to be used again, are the actual ones belonging to those houses, which their grandfathers brought away when sadly turning their faces from that fair and beloved land in 1492.

Except Italian, few languages that one might naturally be supposed to have studied were any help in the white city. Unless Turkish, Arabic, Maltese, modern Greek or desert dialects were part of one's mental equipment, communication proceeded chiefly by pantomime. There were French, Italian and English Consulates, the only European nations having permanent officials in Tripoli; but in the Babel of nationalities overwhelming one's arrival no familiar word was distinguishable.

VI

A Little History

Varied experience has been the portion of Tripoli almost since history began. One of the oldest cities in the world and combining ancient Oea with Leptis Magna and Sabrata, it became Tripolis, "three cities," the "triple town." Possibly founded by Phœnicians several centuries before Christ, little can be traced of its early glory, one-time capital of Syrtica Regio. As Sir Lambert Playfair picturesquely remarks, "All that now remains of the three eastern Barbary states is a bibliography." In those early days its great bay, the Syrtis Major, was considered dangerous to navigation, while beyond lay Ceyrari Barka, that "road of whirlwinds" from Cyrenaica to Egypt, scarcely less threatening in its different menace.

Barbary as a name was thought by Gibbon to be merely continued from the time of its

From the roof of the French Consulate

Roman conquerors, who called barbarian everything outside of their own environment. Other writers think it a repetition of the Arabic word *bar*, meaning desert; or perhaps from Berbers, shepherd dwellers the most ancient of its inhabitants. However the name or country originated, it had a fluctuating and bloody history for centuries.

In A. D. 146 the Emperor Lucius Septimius Severus was born in Tripoli province at Leptis Magna (afterward called Lebda by the Arabs), when Punic was still the language of the country. Severus, that military despot who tolerated no tyranny but his own, was the first Roman emperor who learned Latin as a foreign tongue.

It has passed from Rome to Moslem; from building splendid works of art to beheading statues and throwing them to the ground; from being itself victim of Vandals in the fifth century to its rescue by the Byzantine general Belisarius a century later. Yet in 641 (following the Hejira of 622), when, like a cyclone, Mos-

33

lems and their religion swept from Mecca and
Modena along the African coast, obliterating
all traces of Christianity in their irresistible
progress, Tripoli has not been allowed to remain an unharried stronghold of the prophet.

The Arabs ruled to 787 A. D., after that becoming for a time subject to the rulers of
Tunisia. In 1352 an appeal was sent to Abu
'Ainan, King of Morocco, for fifty thousand
pieces of gold to be used as ransom from the
Genoese — which he dispatched in five loads.
During the reign of Ferdinand V " the Catholic " a Spanish fleet sailed into harbour in 1510
and captured the city in one night. Among the
people of Tripoli is a tradition that the ruins
of a fort standing opposite the Catholic cemetery known as Borg-bu-lela (father of night)
are the remnants of a fortress erected by the
Spanish during that remarkable night. The
better classes in the city refused to recognize
Spanish supremacy, and leaving their homes
many took refuge in near oases, especially
Tajura, which became an important center.

Tajura

A LITTLE HISTORY

Later, about 1528, the ubiquitous Charles V yielded Malta to the Knights of Rhodes, and with it the government of Tripoli, which they held until 1553, but were expelled by the famous Turkish corsairs, Dragut the great, the terrible, and Sinan. The original city walls were attributed to the redoubtable Dragut. He especially knew well why walls were desirable. Some authorities believe they were erected by the Knights, aided by Arab prisoners, and perhaps rebuilt by the corsair. Dragut and Barbarossa scoured the seas with their ships; Dragut, who died fighting for the possession of Malta, is supposed to be buried in or near one of the Tripoli mosques which he founded. As a center for piracy, Tripoli was a great success.

A century later Cromwell, viewing with watchful eye the increased strength of Barbary and the scourge of her pirates, sent in 1655 his Admiral Blake to this troublous region, and heavy chastisement was distributed impartially. Revolts and clashings of different interests and

nations kept the states in a turmoil for generations. One of the Caramanli princes became
governor about 1710. Growing ambitious, he
attempted to become practically independent of
Constantinople, but fearing certain officers,
too loyal to the Sultan, the story goes that
Ahmed Pasha invited them all on one occasion
to a great banquet — from which they never
returned. His successors continued to rule as
Bey for over a century thereafter, the only
period approaching a " golden age " which poor
Tripoli has ever known. The last Caramanli
governor, and probably most famous, was
Jussuf Pasha.

In 1825 a disagreement with Sardinia took
place, and such was the arrogance of Jussuf
Pasha that a fleet was dispatched to reduce him
to terms; he finally submitted, and, in the
words of Dr. Ayra, " meantime the flag of
Savoy was hoisted at the Consulate, and was
saluted by artillery from the forts of Tripoli,
and men were taught to respect the banner
which not long after was destined to float over

the capital, a symbol of Italian unity and liberty." So the autumn of 1911 was not the first time that Italy was conqueror.

The central fort and lighthouse were built on the site of an ancient bastion, now called Burj el-Trab, " earth-fort."

A picturesque incident is related of Abd-el-Mumin, who was hoping to reign after his master, Ibn Tumart. He taught a lion to follow him like a dog, and a bird to say, " Victory and power belong to thee, khalifa Abd-el-Mumin." While the Muwah Hadi council were deliberating on a successor to Ibn Tumart, this lion came rushing in, apparently from the wilds, and crouched at the feet of Abd-el-Mumin. Later the bird appeared and shrieked out its lesson. The effect was magical; opposition vanished, and this clever aspirant was triumphantly elected.

But again the country was conquered. Under the plausible wish of putting an end to disorders occasioned by the ambitions of two brother princes, sons of Jussuf Pasha, Turkey took possession, turning Tripoli into a province or vilayet of her own in 1835.

Since then Tripoli has practically done nothing to foster trade, to improve agricultural methods, to extend irrigation, to enlarge commerce or modernize any art or industry. The Turkish government has been described as more inexorable than the wall of China; and paralyzed by all these conditions, Tripoli has waited, beautiful, picturesque, glowing, but as it were in a state of suspended animation, holding her breath for the next stage. And so the city, oriental in every detail, has been unspoiled by the tourist, and despite loss of trade and importance was still the metropolis for many hundred miles of sparsely inhabited coast line, Mediterranean gateway to the Sahara.

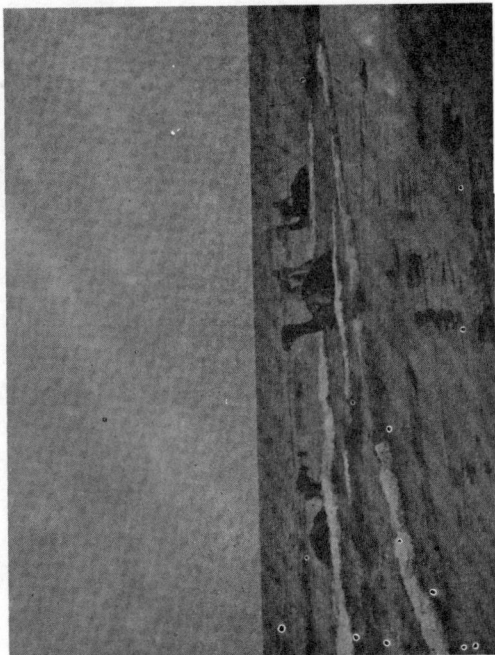

Camels bathing

VII

TRIPOLI AND THE UNITED STATES

The concern of Americans with this far-
away coast began in 1784, near the close of the
Revolution, when pirates were making life
miserable to the newly fledged republic. Our
craft and our diplomatists have not loved
Tripoli for more than a century.

The first aggression by Barbary powers
against the United States and its commerce
appears to have been in October of that year.
Presumably we were sufficiently wearied and
harassed by our own Revolution to fall easy
victims in the Mediterranean to the corsairs
who swept the seas with the greatest danger
and loss of our shipping, to say nothing of our
sailors and officers, many of whom were im-
prisoned, enslaved and most cruelly treated,
in spite of the subsidy paid for protection.

TRIPOLI THE MYSTERIOUS

Treaties were made and broken, and one of the old pamphlets of the time quaintly remarked that Tripoli

" has now fome trade in afhes, oftrich feathers and fkins; but they gain more by the Chriftians taken at fea, for they either fet high ranfoms on them, as we fhall fee in the fequel, in the cafe of our own unfortunate countrymen who have unluckily fallen into their hands, or elfe fell them for flaves."

Our officers made gallant records in these troubled years — Preble, Bainbridge, Decatur and others — but the loss of our frigate, the *Philadelphia,* was a severe blow at a time when we needed all our naval resources. Peace was greatly delayed by this catastrophe, and the large number of prisoners complicated the whole question very seriously. Stories of the imprisonment of our officers in Tripoli are occasionally told there even yet, and picturesque incidents still recounted. Houses were shown me in which the captives were confined, though there was manifest reluctance to talk upon various aspects of this period by the descendants of those concerned.

Houses were shown me where the captives were confined

TRIPOLI AND THE UNITED STATES

In 1804 Tripoli was blockaded by our ships under Commodore Preble, after the loss of the *Philadelphia*, and he, with Bainbridge, conceived the plan of again destroying the frigate, which had been raised and put in commission by the Pasha and his officers. The destroying expedition, in charge of Decatur, was splendidly carried out. The *Philadelphia*, a floating mass of fire, her guns discharging as the flames reached them, finally sank in shallow water near the shore, a complete wreck. Her charred remains could be seen on any quiet day beneath the clear waters of the bay, and a piece of her historic keel now lies on my desk.

This brilliant enterprise added much to the prestige of our navy and was called by the great Nelson "the most bold and daring act of the age." A more perfect outcome, of course, would have been the capture and towing away of the *Philadelphia*, once more to rejoin our own squadron, but the orders of the admiral were explicit. Risks in trying to escape with her were too great.

TRIPOLI THE MYSTERIOUS

Peace was finally restored, and the depredations of the Barbary corsairs ended. Turkey became once more paramount in 1835, and Tripoli has since stood still.

Drill of Arab regiment

VIII

The Pasha's Castle

Once an ancient fortress, this official residence of the Governor was almost a small city in itself. Access to its outer passages was a simple matter for the inhabitants, who thronged its white entrances with petitions, requests or business they thought important, awaiting with stolid patience the time when Turkish soldiers and guardians would admit them to its inner courts. Many of them probably never reached those desired precincts — but they made a picturesque crowd, kept in orderly shape by strict authority.

The chief government offices were located here, the law courts, prisons, warehouses and military stores. There was also a barrack for infantry. Cavalry and artillery were housed farther out of the city. A sort of town council

43

(*beledia*), chosen by the Pasha, had its meetings here. Town finances, street cleaning (the latter, as an Italian writer naïvely remarks, " a function often merely nominal ") and lighting were considered at these times, as well as other city interests. Lighting was not an extraordinarily complicated matter; faint lamps, fed by petroleum, were set here and there in gloomy corners.

The huge structure contained two large courtyards, and was so firmly planted on natural rock that now and again ledges came to the surface in walls and bastion; a few stones with Roman inscriptions occupied corners.

If those dumb walls could speak, centuries of history, unwritten, unremembered, but full of the passion and patriotism, cruelty and treachery of life would be revealed. On one visit to the Pasha he proposed to show us the castle, sending two richly dressed officials as guides. We were not slow to take the implied suggestion of looking only at what was especially designated. It was all intensely inter-

44

His Excellency Redjed Pasha, former Governor of Tripoli

esting, from the Pasha's modern drawing-rooms where delicious coffee and Turkish refreshments were served, to the roof terrace offered as headquarters for our observations overlooking bay and shipping and sands.

On September 1 the anniversary of the Sultan's accession was celebrated with much pomp. Processions and Turkish ceremonies filled the day. In the evening the Pasha gave a brilliant reception. We drove to the Garden gateway over Pianura sands, full of huddled Arabs and sleeping camels. The great pavilion sparkled with lights and decorations, and the Turkish band was playing as we entered. Scarlet and white hangings, divans and embroideries made a gorgeous effect.

Only a few especially invited guests were received within, the immense crowd remaining respectfully outside. We were greeted first by H—— Bey, resplendent in state uniform, and passed on through lines of waiting attendants from one officer to another, and finally to the Pasha himself, who insisted upon our occupying his own special divan and kept us by his side for the remainder of the evening.

Beyond was a private and enclosed garden, where the band was stationed. Ices and coffee, sweets and cake were immediately served, the Pasha chatting volubly to us in Turkish, which was put into excellent French by one of his staff. So the evening passed brilliantly, and the holiday closed with remarkable fireworks as the band played its final tribute to the Sultan.

Turkish and Arab celebration

IX

Inhabitants, Occupations, Schools

Its forty thousand or more inhabitants were hard to disentangle ethnologically; also a reliable census is almost impossible, for under certain interpretations of the Koran its principles oppose such accuracy. Less than five thousand Europeans, chiefly Maltese, were actual residents. The original stock is probably represented by Berbers, but to the onlooker the distinctions between Arab, Moor and Bedouin are slight. A few persons descended from a Turkish father and an Arab mother are termed Corugli or Colugli. So much intermingling of races by marriage as the city showed made still more difficult the task of recognizing nationalities. Many families were crossed Arab-Italian, in such cases usually Mohammedan in belief.

Fezzani and inky Sudanese abounded, many

47

Jews, Italians and Maltese, Albanians in baggy trousers, Greek sponge-divers, Sicilians, whirling dervishes and holy marabouts. Turkish soldiers, lounging in barracks or over the mud walls of their gardens, showed the most diversified rags, and while utterly unkempt and dirty, had generally boyishly honest and amiable faces. Ten thousand troops, chiefly in and near the city, added to its motley and bewildering masses. Only sixteen English-speaking persons lived permanently in Tripoli, and there was no United States Consulate, though one was established in 1910; but the British Consul-General was a host in himself, looking out impartially for the welfare of the most ignorant Maltese, for the extensive English interests in esparto grass and other trade, and for American eclipse expeditions as well. Three postoffices, Turkish, French and Italian, should have given a wonderful ease in transmitting mails. The Italian office served the postal affairs of England. Turkish money being almost hopeless of understanding, our financial transactions

48

Inky Sudanese abounded

were generally conducted in *lire,* though French francs were warmly welcomed.

The numerous esparto *funduks* are characteristic, and we spent entertaining afternoons at a large one owned by an English friend. Piles of sweet-smelling grass lay in tons around the high wall, where an army of black men in all stages of picturesque rags were picking out dead roots and other drawbacks to first quality. Huge piles on their heads, wonderfully balanced, after this process of separation, were carried to a machine, dumped into a sort of iron box, into which two men jumped, packing it hard and solid. Turned by machinery under a steam press, six steel binders were clamped about it until a neatly packed bale ready for shipment finally emerged. Negroes with hooks rolled it off through a gate and up a narrow lane to the storehouse. Tripoli was said to make more than a million francs a year by this export. On its arrival from the interior, the Arab bringing it was paid for weighing and storing, as well as the government tax.

Formerly corn was extensively exported, but when different causes combined to reduce demand, the natives settled down to raise and grind only enough for their own small uses. In various lines much greater activity and prosperity prevailed in earlier times.

Daily life presented a moving picture of nationalities well-nigh unmatched by any other region. Arabs were pervasive, omnipresent; ghostly dream figures muffled in white barracans silently traversed the streets of a pale city equally spectral, the women completely shrouded except one bright black eye, the men showing swarthy faces of inexpressible soberness and dignity. Hurrying Jews, pasty-faced Maltese — the women in the national *faldetta* — and overrunning desert nations filled the highways, in every shade from yellow to deepest brown, thence to dead black like ebony matching their wool, or polished black like patent leather — Berbers, negroes, Fezzani, Sudanese, in a " fluid panorama."

A so-called Turkish college was conducted

A Turkish school for boys

in the city, but the boys had to complete any course of study satisfactorily in Constantinople, especially if intended for a military career. There was a French school for boys conducted by the Marianiste Brothers; also a girls' school and an asylum were carried on by the Sisters of S. Vincent; and there were institutions in charge of the Jewish Union.

A fine collection of meteorological apparatus for use during the 1905 eclipse was installed by Professor Palazzo of Rome on the roof of the Italian school for boys. Italy carried on two elementary schools for boys and for girls, a kindergarten and a technical commercial school with the meteorological observatory attached. The late director of foreign instruction, Sig. Giuseppe Ayra, has given the general meteorological history of Tripoli in a little volume published in Turin several years ago. The observatory established by Italy in 1892 was the only one between Tunis and Alexandria and held a very important position.

The technical school for poor and orphaned

children was housed in a new building, where we were greeted by the grave and competent principal. In the bare reception room Turkish coffee was immediately served. Through many other apartments we were escorted, where boys were working at turning-lathes, and making furniture, machinery and shoes, weaving silk into barracans, dress materials and curtains. The blacksmith shop was equipped with bellows and other appliances exactly like those in use for centuries, and three men were pounding an anvil, making a favourite Arab tune. All colours worked peacefully together, blacks from the Sudan, browns from Misrata and Gabes, lighter tinted Arabs — all races without distinction were amicably friendly.

Across a hot garden, past a paddock full of rams and goats (once an old Arab cemetery), we reached the building where girls were busy at rug-making, and where a demure jet-black maiden had to go ahead to warn the school of our coming, that the little girls, some of whom were old enough to be attractive, might adjust

Bellows . . . exactly like those in use for centuries

their barracans over their faces before the head
of the school and the foreign gentleman should
arrive.   Under ten years the children remained
uncovered.

All turned and saluted us with a charming
manner, and at a signal turned again to their
weaving, which they did with great speed, copy-
ing a design prepared by some supposable
artist. Workmanship was very beautiful, patterns very bad — flags, patriotic insignia and
the map of Africa, with hard outlines and
crudely brilliant colours.

Outside the city are few large centers, and
practically none in the interior. Benghazi, capital of Cyrenaica, near the ruins of ancient
Hesperia (later Berenice), had practically ten
or twelve thousand beside the Turkish garri-
son. But there was no regular communication
either with Europe or Tripoli, sometimes nearly
two months elapsing without this possibility.
Its Governor was of a lower rank than the
Pasha of Tripoli, but still independent of him.
Cyrenaica had only about two hundred thou-

sand inhabitants, and the Italian post-office had often to hold mail for a month or more before any means of forwarding presented itself, English tramp steamers or Turkish transports being the only possible carriers.

At Jebel Gharian a few poor villages clustered about two Turkish fortresses with their garrisons, Kars el-Gharian and Kars el-Jebel. Zentan is the center of an actual troglodyte colony. The inhabitants of these subterranean villages live in shelters cut in the living rock, leaving them only for purposes of labour and harvesting.

X

THE BRITISH CONSULATE–GENERAL

One of the oldest, largest and most interesting dwellings in the city is the official home of England's representative. Built in 1744, a hundred feet square, it surrounds the usual central courtyard and was constructed with reference to repelling a siege. Almost a fortress in itself, it had served purposes of defense and refuge for early dwellers in the uneasy city many times before the English-speaking residents flocked to its shelter in October of 1911. In peaceful times its complicated entrances were occupied only by dozing Arab servants, one of whom, the majestic *cavasse* and interpreter Mufta, would conduct in the expectant visitor whose reason for coming was satisfactory.

Off the court were offices, kitchens and servants' quarters; a huge old tree lifted its branches far above the roof terrace; blossoming shrubs in gracious abundance and the welcome tinkle of water gave a cool and homelike effect to the shady enclosure. Around and above, a gallery was reached by a lovely wrought-iron stairway with sandstone steps, worn into hollows by the feet of a hundred and fifty years. Inviting doorways led to the drawing-rooms and bedchambers, dining-room and boudoirs of the household.

On the gallery wall hung the old national coat-of-arms of Denmark, formerly adorning its own Consulate, afterward abandoned — of especial interest in recalling stories of the humane conduct of a certain Danish Consul toward American prisoners during the wearisome war with Tripoli over a century ago. The insignia of Norway, also weatherbeaten and time-worn, from another Consulate now no more, hung beside the Danish emblem; the slight interests of those countries in this remote Turkish vilayet were being faithfully looked after by the Consul-General for Great Britain, who also

Sandstone steps worn into hollows by the feet of a hundred and fifty
years

represented the few Americans occasionally seeking the shores and sands of Barbary.

Numerous Roman amphoræ and bas-reliefs unearthed from the encroaching sands enriched drawing-rooms and gallery; plants in lavish abundance, bamboo seats and tea-tables made an atmosphere of delightful hospitality.

In its library, a charming place for browsing about, the archives were rich in ancient books and manuscripts. I one day came across the quaintly entertaining volume, " Narrative of a Ten Years' Residence in Tripoli in Africa. From correspondence in possession of Richard Tully, London, 1816." The amusing story told in this old book, of which later editions have been issued but often without the very funny colored plates of the earlier, is contained in letters supposedly written by the wife of a British Consul-General to Lady Mary Wortley Montagu. Many valuable and now all but forgotten details of life in remote Barbary over a hundred years ago are preserved in vivid form by this vivacious lady.

57

TRIPOLI THE MYSTERIOUS

Vehicles used, even well into the nineteenth century, were almost exclusively palanquins enclosed in linen, and mounted upon a camel's back; but these were kept by only a few of the great Moors for their ladies. Others walked. Mourning in Tripoli at this time was denoted more by shabbiness than by distinctive colour — the greater the grief, the more careless one's dress. A new article, necessarily purchased, was dragged through water to take off its first freshness before wearing.

One pamphlet, printed in 1806, described quaintly the " Tripoline " war of the United States. Another, far older and very rare, I afterward found in the British Museum:

" Late Newes out of Barbary. In a letter written of late from a Merchant there, to a Gentleman not long fince employed into that Countrie from his Maiestie. Containing fome ftrange particulars, of this new Saintifh Kings proceedings: as they have been very credibly related from fuch as were eye-witneffes. Imprinted at London for Arthur Jonfon. 1613."

BRITISH CONSULATE–GENERAL

But far more entertaining than any published book was the manuscript journal kept by
H. M.'s representative in Tripoli between 1768
and 1772. He begins promptly:

"The man of war that cary's me anchor'd in ye
road att Tripoly ye King's ship to fire an evening
gun at setting ye watch.

"Memorandum to inquire what is to be done
about ye additional salute. All ye Consuls will
visit me promis. without observing any order upon
my arrival, preceded by a message deliver'd by a
Dragoman. I can return none of these visits till
I have presented my Credentials to ye Bashaw.
When I visit ye Bashaw by his appointment that
part of ye presents intended for him must be
carry'd with me, that part of ye presents for his
officers I distribute att my own convenience . . .
I shall find ye Bashaw sitting; the form of salu-
tation is to advance and kiss his write and left
cheek and make him a bow. I sett on his left side,
being the place of honour in Tripoly.

"To make my first visit alone.

"To take care y^t I am saluted with 7 Guns
being my privilidge. Ye Capt may if he pleases return ye salute. . . . The Choux or Civil officer that
always presents ye Bashaw's present of refreshments to be each day entertained on board ship
with coffee and Capilaire in ye wardroom, not in

ye Captain's cabin, every day when he leaves ye ship the Choux must be saluted with 3 Guns only no Turks whatever on makeing a visit should be saluted. . . . By this time or probably sooner I shall be apply'd to for payment of 4 zequins for the salute made according to treaty to his Majesty's ship on her arrival. This salute is due by treaty and not to be paid for. They will ask for 4 zequins for my being saluted . . . for which there is no necessity. . . . Ye Captain of ye Port in particular and many other Turks will without any shame ask for anything on board ye ship or in my house . . . but there is no necessity for giving them everything they ask for."

Then follow directions to himself as to the orders relative to flags.

" Ye hoisting of His Majesty's colours upon different occasions becomes a kind of Publick Language perfectly well understood by Moors as well as Christians,"

and proceeding to emphasize the fact that the " colours must be kept chaste " to ensure respect, he gives a list of occasions when they may with propriety be hoisted.

Att Christmas 3 Days. Every Sunday in ye year. Saint George's Day new stile and old stile. Easter

Monday. Fourth June His Majesty's birthday.
N. B. Ye first visit rec'd from and pay'd to every
Consul. Ye same when I introduce any person of
condition to them or receive their visits or return
any publick or cerem. dinner given or rec'd, the
birth of a child to any Consul, the birthday of his
Prince kept by any Consul when desir'd, whenever
the Bashaw or his Elder Son rides out, 2 publick
feast days of Byram and Ramadan, the birth of a
Prince or Princess of the Ottoman port, the first
visit pay'd to me by an ambassador appointed by the
Bashaw to any European court after he is appointed
and when he embarks, wh. is twice and no more."

For times and persons when it is quite un-
necessary to waste the honour, a careful list
follows; and after remarking that at the feasts
of Byram and Ramadan it has been usual to
make presents, this long-gone official adds
naïvely, " wee have great ships and need make
none."

He also writes of the pushing and crowding
of Consuls in calling on the Bashaw, as to " who
shall gett first," but since the representative
of His Majesty has always had precedence, " it
never can be necessary for him to put himself

on a footing of having a scramble." As to calling upon the first Treasurer, " this is an inno-
vation and therefore a compliment to be paid
him or not as he behaves. They will all offer
coffee of a bad kind and without sugar. I must
taste it att each house notwithstanding, it being
a mark of enmity to refuse a dish of coffee
when offered by a Turk."

Immensely entertaining notes follow about
" oyl" and provisions, markets and seasons,
and a "red wine from the Mediterranean cost
of France, drinks like claret att first, but sowers
presently." Caravans and ostrich feathers,
gold, senna, snuff; from Mecca silks, muslins,
coloured stones, pearls, small Persian carpets;
and black slaves exported to Constantinople, all
receive careful annotation at the hand of this
conscientious gentleman, who seems to have
had a clear brain for everything but spelling.
That he was energetic to the last would appear
to be shown by an added note, written by a
later, evidently admiring, hand, " He died in his
breeches."

BRITISH CONSULATE–GENERAL

Both in spring and the height of summer Tripoli air was full of inspiration. Even when the *gibleh* blew, bringing a fine golden haze of sand from close-creeping Sahara spaces, with air hot and dry like a furnace, it was scarcely less full of the wine of life than when the sea wind came in from the Mediterranean, rippling the water to deep indigo flecked by whitecaps. Rain water at certain seasons is conducted from the constantly whitewashed roofs to cisterns below, where may be stored the year's supply.

After the sun slipped down from the blazing heavens and shadows grew long and cool, roof terraces became the city's promenades where veiled ladies emerged, white like the city itself, to gaze safely forth above curious eyes.

A broad expanse of terrace at the Consulate, higher than any other edifice in the city except its minarets, afforded delightful evening quarters, far above the shouts and confusion of the narrow masonry cañons below. Every afternoon when tea in the pretty drawing-room was over, and the intense sunlight began to come in level and less burning rays, I always spent an hour or two on the roof.

Too hot and blinding for use during the day, the terraces were more and more charming as sunset drew on. The white glare was subdued to pleasant lightness, and all humanity mounted to its lovely vantage grounds for breathing space, open prospect, star-gleam.

In the narrow streets donkeys and camels and Arabs passed and repassed; bakers with their round and shining loaves, in yellow heaps just out of the oven, better as decoration than sustenance, Cretans, Albanians, Maltese, promiscuously mingled; and street cries ascended with their emphatic, unintelligible enunciation, constantly reiterated.

Later the west grew yellow and magnificent, a sort of widespread radiance, hinting greater possibilities in reserve. The seventeen-domed mosque stood out whitely, even in that city of whiteness, the sapphire Mediterranean lapped serenely on the beach, the gleaming desert

64

The seventeen-domed mosque stood out whitely, even in that city of whiteness

stretched mysteriously into dim twilight space, quiet palms rested their plumes from rustling.

Then out upon the minarets, just beneath the ultimate green summits, each crowned by its golden crescent, emerged the white-draped muezzins, shrouded in ghostly barracan, for their fifth daily call of the faithful to prayer, white as the towers on which they stood and seeming hardly more human. Looking first into the sky, they bent low over the parapet, sending forth the call, singularly penetrating, and audible for long distances, albeit the voices have no real resonance and are hopelessly " squeezed " in quality.

After dinner a still later phase came on, when roofs, domes, towers were suddenly flooded with the lighthouse flash close by, which hardly dimmed a full-moon brightness. It might have been a fairy city, beautiful beyond imagining. A palm tree showed here and there, from some hidden courtyard, gaining dark value in the silver scene, and tinkling music ascended, with no melody and no rhythm, a part of all the vague and ghostly yet exquisite beauty. Toward the shore hooded monks in brown habit and rope girdle promenaded the roof of the Roman Catholic church — a foreign, not an integral part of the oriental evening.

Glorified dust, whirling swallows, calls to sunset devotion, the silent desert close-clasping, on-coming moonlight, the coolness and blossom odour — these were Tripoli.

XI

THE ROMAN ARCH AND ANCIENT REMAINS

Enticing as the native life of modern times
proved — homely ancestral arts, picturesque
decay, thronging tribes — more suggestive,
pathetic, absolutely engrossing, was the omnipresent evidence of a splendid period long
since perished. The whole region is rich in
ruins, edifices, tombs, arches, columns, pavements, sculpture in scattered fragments, great
aqueducts, but all covered by resistlessly moving desert sands or whitewashed, blurred and
broken, spoiled by carelessness, ignorance,
fanaticism. The grandeur of that long-gone age
cannot be concealed even by such wholesale
slaughter of the beautiful. Despite the ravages
of time and the deplorable neglect of man, even
in mutilation the ruin still bears noble witness to
a civilization which once held the world captive.

Exquisite slabs of carved marble are made to

67

do duty as doorsteps; stones with half-effaced inscriptions are built into countless cheap and sordid walls; and at the intersection of two narrow and lane-like streets, Shara Erbat Saat and Suk el-Yahud el-Hararah, four fine Roman pillars performed the part of corner posts.

The most superb relic of these ancient days now departed is the four-sided triumphal arch, said to extend no less than twenty feet below the street level and reaching more than the same height above, wherein a wine shop and coal store hold gayly forth, yet obliterating only in part the magnificence of their incongruous shelter.

Built by a loyal Roman citizen at the head of the Customs in A. D. 164, it was erected in honor of the Emperor Marcus Aurelius. Such parts of the splendid structure as were yet visible above general rubbish were seen to be carved in relief, and the whole, even in degradation, shows the vast conception and characteristic solidity of construction which can smile on the centuries and calmly withstand the buffetings of nature and far more cruel man.

The most superb relic . . . is the four-sided triumphal arch

ROMAN ARCH, ANCIENT REMAINS

"Victory," a graceful female figure, stands in a car drawn by two winged sphinxes; various trophies of arms may still be traced, a Roman eagle on a helmet, and the Latin inscription: —

IMP · CAES · M · AVRELIO · ANTONIN · AVG · P · P · ET · IMP · CAES · L · AVRELIO · VERO · ARMENIACO · AVG ·

SER · CORNELIVS · ORFITVS · PROCOS · CVM · VITTEDIO · MARCELLO · LEG · SVO · DEDICAVIT ·

C · CALPVRNIVS · CELSVS · CVRATOR · MVNERIS · PVB · MVNERARIVS · II · VIR · QQ · FLAMEN · PERPETVVS ·

ARCVM · PECVNIA · SVA · LOCO · PVBLICO · A · FVNDAMENTIS · EX · MARMORE · SOLIDO · FECIT · [1]

Several words in the last line are nearly obliterated. The African fondness for whitewash which buries carvings, Moorish tiles, beauty of all kinds beneath its deadly touch, has not spared the noble arch, of course; and all the

[1] Full text and translation of the inscription have been kindly supplied by my husband's colleague, Dr. Houghton:

Imperatori Caesari Marco Aurelio Antonino Augusto patri patriae et Imperatori Caesari Lucio Aurelio Vero Armeniaco Augusto Servius Cornelius Orfitus proconsul cum Vittedio Marcello legato suo dedicavit. Caius Calpurnius Celsus curator muneris publici munerarius duumvir quinquennalis flamen perpetuus arcum pecunia sua loco publico a fundamentis ex marmore solido fecit.

Servius Cornelius Orfitus proconsul, together with Vittedius Marcellus his lieutenant [legatus], dedicated [this arch] to the imperial Caesar Marcus Aurelius Antoninus Augustus, father of his Country, and to the imperial Caesar Lucius Aurelius Verus Armeniacus Augustus. Caius Calpurnius Celsus, keeper of the public funds, bestower of gifts, duumvir quinquennalis, flamen for life, erected [this] arch in a public place, built of solid marble from the foundations, at his own expense.

"Munerarius," *a giver of public games.* "Quinquennalis," *holding office for five years.* "A "flamen" was a priest of one particular deity. Fourth line of the inscription literally: *arch at his own expense in a public place from the foundations of solid marble he made.* Corpus Inscriptionum Latinarum, viii, I, 24 reads VTTEDIO instead of VITTEDIO.

time stealthy desert sands have drifted in, burying more and more of the stately relic as years go on. But it gave veritable heartache to see so majestic a structure subject to the vandal touch of ignorance so consummate.

Well-preserved pavements are found outside the city, and evidence is everywhere apparent even to the most casual that remains of a once triumphal Roman occupation are but superficially overlaid by the sordid life of a polyglot community, lacking all appreciation for the stately memorials of a magnificent past.

Mr. H. S. Cowper's book, entitled " The Hill of the Graces," contains much valuable information on all the ancient remains, which he visited and studied as carefully as a watchful government allowed. Oases, deserts, sand dunes, all tell, perhaps blindly and unwillingly, but none the less certainly, a story centuries old, half forgotten, overlaid, yet patiently waiting interpretation.

Mr. Cowper considers many of the *senams* as far older than Roman days, finding traces

even of a prehistoric stone age, in a remarkable
series of megalithic monuments which he com-
pares with Stonehenge; he believes it not impossible that the worship of the trilithonic
symbol may even have made its way from
Africa to Salisbury Plain. The *senams*, a
word in Arabic meaning " idol," are door-like
structures of dressed stone, a characteristic
feature of the ruins, and may have originated
with a race living here long before the Roman
annexation of Regio Tripolitana.

Probably the climate differed in those far-
away days, as certain faint indications show.
There is a popular belief in the city that opening the Suez Canal is perhaps the chief cause.
There was certainly more wooded country, containing more streams which later and more
careless inhabitants have allowed to perish.
At present there is not one perennial stream
properly called a river. In the rainy season
many a *wadi* or river-bed fills with a rushing tide; and when in February of 1904 a
cloudburst nearly submerged the city, all the

71

sandy lanes became torrent beds, bringing much devastation.

If all the ruined temples were in use at any one time, the population of Tarhuna and M' Salata must have equaled London at least. Even if some of them were built in different ages, the numbers must have been very great. There are fine ruins at Garia el-Sergia and Garia el-Garbia, south and west of Tripoli. Farther in the same direction are Zellah and Tirsa, where ostriches are raised. For long years all digging for archæological material was forbidden by the Turkish government, as already mentioned, but despite restrictions a good deal of quiet investigation went on; and of Roman remains, fine if headless statues often came to light, bas-reliefs of much magnificence, inscriptions and columns in good condition after long burial in the sands.

Near Homs, a center for the export of halfa, or esparto, a sort of grass much used for matting and paper, are the ruins of Leptis Magna (Lebda), founded by Sidonians only a

The ruins of Leptis Magna

century after Rome, and for a time a rival of
Carthage herself. The principal ruins of
Lebda lie about the mouth of a small stream
or what should be a stream (*wadi* Lebda).
On account of rabid vandalism, not only Arab
but European, little remains of its early splen-
dor. It is said that in the eighteenth century
Louis XIV obtained from the government of
Tripoli permission to export to Paris whatever
he chose from Lebda. Many priceless columns
adorn the church of S. Germain-des-Près.

According to a pamphlet on North Africa
by Lieutenant-Commander Gorringe, United
States Navy, published by the American Geographical Society in 1881, Admiral Smyth of
the English Navy removed many more, afterward placed in the Royal Gardens at Windsor.
Those remaining, which should have been
matchless memorials of a great past, have been
mutilated and destroyed by vandalism not
wholly Arabic. Enough may yet be seen, however, to show the dignity and glory of that
early city.

XII

To the Caves

An hour or two from Tripoli, near Ghirgaresh, are curious caves which might once
have sheltered an army of troglodytes. Camels
were decidedly the best conveyance, but we
once had excellent donkeys for the trip, and
at another time tried the bone-racking *araba,*
whose merry curtains effectively kept out all
breezes and conserved the heat to a discour-
aging extent.

Out of the city through narrow lanes between high mud walls, over which pomegranate and Barbary fig, gray olive and plumy
palm waved and blossomed or offered fruit
and shade, into the sand of the " Tunis road "
we plunged. Here and there the winds had
blown bare underlying rock, " the bleached
bones of the world " unwittingly protruding in

Into the sand of the "Tunis road" we plunged

grooves, ridges and gullies. Palms accentu-
ated the dazzling landscape. Without this all-
important tree, desert and oasis life would be
well-nigh impossible. Kindling wood and
building material from its trunk, baskets,
ropes, brushes from the branches, the date
palm supplies also the chief article of food,
shade as well as fans, and *lakbe,* an intoxicating beverage.

There was no real road, but the route lay
along the shore past several beautiful domes of
marabout tombs. These smaller domes over
the bones of holy men are numerous in all the
city environs. Each is frequently covered with
bright flags brought by Moslem women when
a longed-for happiness has come, or when some
one near and dear has recovered from illness.

Old wells, guardians of walled gardens, appeared frequently between sea and desert, each
giving its oddly vocal squeak as the goatskin
was let down empty or pulled up filled, cow
and man gravely walking up and down the hill
together. Each garden was carefully watched

75

and tended. The Arabs have a proverb that no palm tree will bear unless it hears daily the voice of its owner.

One of the numerous Turkish forts lay in this direction, where idle soldiers in bright red sashes and picturesque rags lounged over their mud barricades and peeped through cactus hedges. Poor fellows! Their life was the acme of monotony. Belted and befezzed, even the passing of half a dozen strangers was of interest in a day devoid of incident.

Just here a sharp skirmish was fought with the Italians late in 1911, which successfully banished monotony.

Before reaching Ghirgaresh a strange, probably pre-Mohammedan, ruin rises from the sand high into modern sunlight in singular isolation. Its story is untold, its crumbling walls full of the echoes of a wonderful past for him who can interpret. What mysterious uses could this ancient stronghold have had, lacking doors and windows and steps or any means of entrance? This place is mentioned by Leo Africanus;

Marabout and palm

One of the caves at Ghirgarish

and the Arabs say the Emir Kerakish built it
— which might show the derivation of the
name. One of our drivers, Balaid, pulled himself up by fingers and toes to the summit, looking down smilingly from that elevation, but
without adding much to an intelligent solution
of the mystery.

Under the road near by was a large vaulted
chamber for unknown purposes, possibly used
as stables in olden days. At our entrance dis-
gusted and expostulatory owls flew out with
whoops and a great flapping of heretofore un-
disturbed wings. Beyond and ever beyond lay
an eternity of sand, drifting, restless, covering
dead ruins and living gardens with equal devastation, silent and resistless.

In these barren lands I counted twenty-six
kinds of wild flowers, though a casual glance
would have pronounced the region absolutely
without vegetation. Nearly all were small and
low, though occasional large masses of a lovely
purple flower set in thick leaves wafted an
odour like catnip or mint. Some of its blossoms

77

were entirely white. The tiniest of morning-glories grew in a thick tuft; there were yellow blossoms like small thistles with prickly leaves; an infinitesimal dandelion appeared, and a charming, bright blue, five-petaled flower of some entirely new species, a smaller one of the same exquisite azure, with a corolla like a forget-me-not, only growing in clusters, many blossoms on one stem; and a brilliant crimson tube, turning dull purple as it faded. All made a veritable wild garden in a savage wilderness easily overlooked unless one carefully searched.

Suddenly, sunk in an apparently level moorland, were unexpected depressions, like deep holes, down which we climbed to find ourselves before huge caves, in all over fifty, where the air was cool and dry, a different world from that of the scorching sunlight above. In texture like hardened sand, the rock was nevertheless exceedingly solid, apparently waterworn, in places grotesquely shaped, some of the caves of natural origin, others quite prob-

Some of the caves of natural origin, others . . . old quarries

ably old quarries. Low, flat arches led still farther down and in, made centuries ago by human hands. More modern workmen had chiseled other marks and removed huge blocks of stone. Swallows and bats protested madly at our intrusion, and while we studied the strange pillars, arches, ceilings and inscriptions, our Arabs spread a delicious luncheon, subsequently scouring the dishes thriftily in sand. They have learned not to waste precious water superfluously.

On one of these trips the French Consul was our host, and with us rode the French astronomer Libert.

The caves are very near the sea, and sunset effects were remarkable on water-worn rocks, gentle surf and far reaches of sand toward the white city itself in rosy distance.

XIII

WELLS AND GARDENS

Primitive wells for irrigating gardens are scattered about, a patient cow walking all day up and down a little hill, letting an empty goatskin into cooling depths, only to bring it overflowing to the surface. The goatskin, or leather bottle, is shaped like a funnel, closed at the narrow end, and lowered by ropes over rough wooden cylinders, themselves supported by masonry pillars nine or ten feet high. A cow, the all-day motive power, is hardly more patient than the faithful attendant Arab. There are said to be approximately more than eight thousand wells in Tripoli and its environs, but owing to Arabic dislike of accurate estimate, the actual number may be even greater.

Every garden had its well and simple system

Every garden had its well

of irrigation, and high mud walls against the
ever-encroaching sand. Over the dull gray
barrier scarlet pomegranate blossoms, oleander,
palms, even climbing roses peeped at the passer
below, hinting of lavish joys within. But anti-
quated methods had never been superseded,
and ambition was unknown. Even lubrication
of the simple well-apparatus was neglected, and
each had its distinctive squeak — one a high
G, others giving different tones, occasionally
two or three in succession, making little melodies all their own. A blind man might have
learned to know his whereabouts by these
pseudo-tunes and their variations.

Certain old Latin authors have written of
the marvelous fertility of the soil; and only a
little water and comparatively slight labor
would now be needed for abundant yield.
Date palms were of course the chief reliance,
but olives, pomegranates, oranges, bananas and
apricots grew luxuriantly; and we were frequently offered excellent native watermelons.

A sad little sight on the outskirts was a tiny

garden whose owner must have died, for the wall had fallen in a dozen breaks and had not been repaired. The well was silent, the reservoir empty. Through every opening the piled-up sand was drifting, drifting, and the desert had almost claimed its own. Yet a few flowers and fruits still struggled on, obviously worsted, certain to be ultimately overwhelmed, but thrusting pathetically hopeful blossoms and fresh leaves above their silent and resistless foe.

The gardens of wealthy Arabs, both Jewish and Mohammedan, were veritable beauty spots, luxuriant and magnificent. Always a central pond, with goldfish and fountain, surrounded by blossoming water-plants, formed the reservoir from which small irrigating canals traversed the whole garden space, where flowers bloomed lavishly and golden oranges filled the trees. One could imagine himself in a semi-tropical region of the utmost richness, where no memory of the ever-moving, tireless sand could intrude. But the high mud wall has only to present the smallest break for doom to enter.

Tripoli gardens should form a small volume in themselves, beginning with a description of the great Turkish garden where the band discoursed astonishing music every afternoon, while we took our afternoon tea—or coffee—in a pretty pavilion or in the shade of palm trees.

Late one afternoon we drove out by invitation to the country place of a wealthy Arab, whose garden was famous. Past the well-remembered and mysterious black holes which go down to unknown depths, supposed to be ancient *silos,* or places for cutting up grain and food for animals, we reached the airy villa of our aim. High walls completely shut away the outside world. Brilliant zinnias were in full blossom, dahlias and geraniums, with the usual orange and fig trees, olive and lemon, pomegranates and palm. Our host was much interested in what American gardens could produce, and asked for minute descriptions of such flowers as he did not know.

83

TRIPOLI THE MYSTERIOUS

Lanes and roads leading out of the city to the gardens were endlessly attractive and newly delightful each time we drove or ambled down their sandy ways. Enormous old cactus plants, often quite trees, crowned high and frequently crumbling walls, over which gray olives swung. Splendid horses, sumptuously decorated with silver and leather, with long, flowing tails, bearing companies of Arabs or Turks, were liable to be met in the narrowest lanes, as well as droves of camels, donkeys or goats.

Decaying adobe mosques, marabouts, villages, were passed as we went onward into the open one late afternoon, and to the highest hill in Tripoli, which gave a wide view over miles of palms off to the desert. Two men were winnowing grain by tossing it up from a flat basket for the wind to blow away the chaff, a method used by farmers in New England less than a century ago. Up the bare hill slope we rode where the wind blew with a lonely swish across the red, hard-baked hillside. By

Lanes and roads leading out of the city

more narrow lanes we veered across a rather
pleasant, because partly irrigated, country,
with olive trees and bright green lucerne, to
the Jewish village, Amrus.

Most of the men were blacksmiths, and had
brought from the shore all manner of old
anchors of huge proportions to work over into
implements. A closely built village with adobe
houses treading on each other's toes in the
narrowest of streets — though there is all out-
doors to expand in — the synagogue, finest of
their buildings, was open for evening prayers.

The " oven " was central meeting ground for
men, women, babies and all, and here in the
fitful firelight much gossip was going on, as all
clustered about to watch the baking. A stone
showing a half-obliterated Roman inscription
was in use as a seat, and large round platforms
of masonry held stone rollers for crushing
olives collected from the orchards all about.
Oil is made in the most primitive manner
possible.

From the open country, returning sunset

drives formed one of our loveliest experiences. Facing the wonderful yellow west, palms, mosques and minarets were drawn against it in enchanting silhouette; homeward-bound Arabs, swathed in white, were riding small donkeys or perched on camels, pretty boys trudging beside them through the sand. And ever the golden glory grew until, suddenly paling, stars pricked through the crystalline dome of that marvelous African firmament, though mysterious illumination still came from somewhere on ghostly mosque and tower, but all else faded into soft night. As it grew darker, faint lights shone dimly through crevices of roadside tombs, the plaintive iteration of the wells ceased, and we were once more absorbed into the narrow city streets.

Returning sunset drives

XIV

HAREMS AND COURTYARDS

Every house, even the simplest, had its open
courtyard, a sort of *patio,* around which the
family rooms opened, thus preserving that non-
committal, blank aspect toward the street so
characteristic of oriental dwellings. From the
fair vantage point of the Consulate roof terrace one might look straight down into many
a little courtyard where children and mothers,
dogs and cats, had slept and eaten, rolled, tumbled and lived a daylight programme. Here
and there such a home spot was almost roofed
by passion-flower vines in full blossom.
Strange tinkling music ascended, and a happy
if restricted life filled them with a certain sort
of pleasantness all day — deserted at evening
for the clear space above.

Many of the harem courtyards were well

paved, the wainscot also of handsome tiles, and there was always a central fountain, or fine tree, and blossoming shrubs. On a visit of invitation to one of the best harems, I found the chief wife ill, but she sent for us to her room. In a graceful sort of night drapery she received us, wearing huge earrings and rings, her hair tied up in a blue silk scarf, and reclining on straw mats raised one step above the floor. She had a pleasant face and spoke intelligently on various simple subjects. Coffee was served at once.

No moving air can penetrate those dark interior rooms of which the single barred window opens off the court. In this particular home the big airy chambers above, reached by the gallery, were given to the eldest son and his new wife. Taste in furnishing was execrable, and worse almost in proportion to the amount of money spent. Cheap European finery and tinsel seemed taking the place of earlier and better oriental forms and colours.

Another day I went to a house of quite different social order, where a poor woman with

Many of the harem courtyards were well paved, the wainscot also of handsome tiles

a crooked spine had asked to see the foreigner..
She was sewing at a little machine low on the
floor, turned by hand, like those used by
Malays, her knees higher than her head — but
that was apparently a favourite attitude of both
sexes. A young woman sat near nursing her
baby, a forlorn, feebly wailing mite. Her first
child sat out on the courtyard flagging, with
the usual diseased eyes and trouble with its
skin. Flat on the floor lay an old woman
sound asleep, merely a neighbour in for a while,
to take this surprising means of promoting
social hilarity. But she wore a good deal of
jewelry, was artistically tattooed, and, upon
waking, showed strong, short white teeth in a
friendly smile. The natives seemed to take
little care of their teeth, yet preserved them
well into old age. I do not remember to have
seen a toothless Arab.

The poor little deformed woman seemed
pathetically glad to see us, and began to talk at
once of the coming eclipse, of her fear that it
might injure her, and that she should not dare
go to the roof to see it; also asking me to use

my influence to render it as harmless as possible.

The various wives in each home were apparently on good terms with one another, though each kept more or less to her own apartments in the better families. Children played amicably together, to whichever mother they might belong.

A forest of thread hung up to dry after being dyed decorated another *patio*, and a pretty girl was winding reels and bobbins in the shade. An old woman was similarly employed; and another was combing rough lambs' wool with several kinds of spiked brushes. The chief room was full of gold Turkish embroideries in pillows, cushions and divans, and ornamenting the wall. Heavily curtained beds occupied the end, one above another.

Generally the courtyards were fairly clean and often beautifully paved, though whitewashing had nearly covered most of the wall-tiles. At one house a middle-aged woman sat on the platform sifting queer flour through a

Sudanese village — Tripoli across the bay

series of sieves. Ultimately the chaff was
separated from the coarse flour, that in turn
from the finer. A fat woman was washing
clothes in a big, shallow bowl on the floor, bend-
ing quite double from the hips to reach it. No
reason was apparent why she should not have
had it set up on something. A rather attractive
young girl was crocheting lace, while a wizened
little old woman made an incredibly small bundle of herself, grinding coffee in a tiny brass
mill. Children were, as usual, scattered about
promiscuously. All the women were heavily
laden with necklaces and bracelets; huge earrings (gold and silver circles) were often hung
from three or four holes in each ear. One
young married woman was elaborately self-
tattooed. Shoes were removed to go into the
open rooms, and a white sheepskin was brought
for us to sit upon.

Industrious and fairly happy they all seemed,
with a good deal more of the home-making
spirit and atmosphere than might have been
anticipated.

XV

'ARAB WEDDINGS

The peculiar sound indicating joy, or a happy event about to take place, filled the narrow streets. It was shortly after midnight, and my first nap was at its deepest.

The day had been a busy one, filled with visits in harems, ending with a Consulate dinner and coffee at the Marina. At first the strange cry but dimly pierced consciousness. Then I woke more fully, and running to the window over the chilly stone floor, climbed into its wide embrasure and looked out. The weird cry continued to fill the darkness, and a large crowd had gathered, servants with flaring torches marching ahead of two or three open carriages, drawn by fine Arabian horses — equipages unusual enough in themselves in 1900 to have attracted excited attention. Within the first sat a lady wrapped in a lovely

92

white silk barracan, two black women servants with her, to whose elastic throats the penetrating tremolo was due. Behind came other servants and carriages, the procession followed by a motley crowd of onlookers.

This joyful company proved to consist of the mother of a prospective bridegroom, who with her servants and friends was announcing to the world that a new daughter-in-law was about to come to her home.

The sound itself is made far back in the throat by women who add a strange and penetrating quiver, almost impossible to copy, a weirdly joyous effect indescribable. The same sound is made for other kinds of approaching good, as when some old person has at last saved money enough to get to Mecca and is about to start. He or she always hopes that death may come in the sacred city, one old woman I saw just leaving for her journey being pathetically eager to get there before her failing limbs should utterly collapse.

The glad tidings of an imminent wedding

93

thus announced, the next night (Thursday, a favorite night for weddings) another and larger procession filled the streets usually so quiet, men in ghostly barracans leading the merry-makers. Following were numerous blacks, Sudanese from the south, beating drums, burning red fire and letting off something in the nature of firecrackers; a company of small boys marched at the side bearing aloft lanterns and torches. The happy bridegroom walked in the midst, taking this cheerful farewell of bachelorhood. For hours the parading victim and his friends traversed the streets in general jollification, ended by his giving them a fine banquet toward three in the morning at some café or public house.

While these obvious events were in progress on the second night, the bride was being quietly conveyed by her friends to the bridegroom's house, with a less noticeable flourish of trumpets but none the less jubilee, and placed in charge of his mother. She had probably never seen her prospective lord or any other man ex-

Street of arcades, castle in background

cept her father and young brothers since early childhood. No girl older than twelve or thirteen goes into the street even shrouded, nor until she has been some time married; and she may not, of course, see any man but the nearest home relatives in the domestic courtyard.

The two families had arranged this suitable match. They were of similar social and financial standing, and everything was perfectly understood and agreeable to all concerned. During Thursday, occasionally the day before, the bridegroom will have gone to the mosque for certain formalities, but it is never necessary for the bride to appear there.

On Friday occurs the real celebration — that part of the ceremony most interesting to the visitor; and to this I was formally bidden, a summons not to be lightly regarded. One of the best houses in Tripoli, the central courtyard was finely paved with pale green tiles, balconies and woodwork matching the same delicate shade. Windows and open doorways gave access to the rooms within; and all available space — galleries, rooms, court — was filled with female friends of the high con- ·tracting parties.

In a line around the sides sat forty or fifty women, attractively youthful in aspect, but powdered to ghastly whiteness, and with vivid crimson triangles painted on either cheek. Their eyebrows were heavily emphasized in black, meeting above the nose and extending across the temples to the hair. Brilliant ani- line dyes, so dearly loved in the East that they have nearly superseded the soft old vegetable colours of a more artistic past, appeared in dazzling combination. Short skirts, full trou- sers, blouses, sleeveless jackets, silk and velvet, all thickly embroidered in gold and silver, showed every conceivable colour — crimson, pink, scarlet, yellow, cobalt-blue, grass-green — until brocades and gauze, flowers, chains, bracelets, all melted into one bewildering whole, overpoweringly brilliant, gaudy, theatrical.

The little bride, rigidly immovable as the changeless etiquette of centuries has decreed, center of all eyes, sat in a conspicuous position among these very gorgeous attendant ladies, herself more magnificent than any, a veritable riot of colour. Her velvets and silks in trousers and blouse, the silver gauze floating from her tightly braided black hair, the brocade vest, gilt slippers, pounds of earrings hanging from half a dozen holes in each ear, yards of golden sequins wound about her slender throat, and equal yards of flower corollas woven in chains, and depending in festoons about her white and crimson cheeks — each was bigger or longer or brighter or heavier than those of the others, as indeed was quite fitting for this one great epoch in her life.

Utterly quiet indeed sat the youthful bride, her hands, henna-dyed to reddish blackness, painted with gold in conventional pattern to the wrist, outspread upon her knees, while a lady at each side fanned her with assiduous devotion in the breathless heat. No turn of the head or motion of an eyelid indicated that she was aware of her exalted position, and when

97

the sun, creeping around in his downward path, sent one straight arrow-shaft directly into her face, not a wink or blink disturbed her open-eyed composure. The two nearest attendants, however, after anxiously looking at one another for an instant, appeared to come to the unanimous decision that this was an occasion demanding heroic action; and gently pushing the bride to an upright position, placed one of her feet before the other, bearing most of her weight upon their own shoulders, and finally succeeded in steering her across the courtyard to a seat on the shady side, like a particularly stiff-jointed doll.

Meantime black women from the desert, seated flat upon the tiled floor, continued to beat upon tom-toms and pound cymbals, accompanied by a most barbarous chant, which appeared to give great satisfaction to the guests, most of whom were regaling themselves at bowls of *cus-cus* and other delicacies, each with her long-handled spoon.

During certain hours for three days this sitting

in state would continue, and for a month or more the new daughter-in-law would be the guest of honour, waited upon, watched with much attention, and allowed no part in work or worry.

The bridal chamber was very magnificent with rugs and divans, gold-embroidered pillows, curtains, the walls draped with oriental hangings — and everywhere were women and babies and toddling children, examining, eating, laughing, contented, joyous.

The bride's father had had the four regulation wives, and was once the proud parent of over fifty children, but only about fourteen had lived beyond babyhood: a small family for Mohammedan Tripoli, as he sadly told me on another occasion.

Most picturesque of all the figures among the wedding guests were three or four Bedouins from the desert, brown-faced, dark-eyed women, the impress of weather upon their russet-red cheeks, and hands and arms, hair and throats were weighted with silver chains, their ears heavy with silver ornaments, a lifetime's wealth. They seemed intensely interested in the lighter-haired stranger and her peculiar clothes, intimating by quite intelligible signs that they would like to have their pictures taken with the little camera they noticed under her arm, posing themselves like eager children.

I had hoped to get a few photographs of this striking scene, but had not attempted it, knowing the superstitious feeling of many Arabs on the subject. Now, however, I spoke to the hostess, the bridegroom's mother, through my companion, an English lady accomplished in Arabic, and asked if I might be permitted to take a photograph or two.

After a moment of interpreting, her meaning was quite clear — there was no objection to my taking anything so long as I omitted the bride; she was quite sure her son would not like his new wife's face to be caught in a camera: otherwise I might take what I chose. The light, however, was already waning, so that I exposed but three films; and bidding adieu to the festive scene, I retreated.

ARAB WEDDINGS

That evening as we were finishing our dinner about eight o'clock, came a distracted Arab gentleman of charming manners but much perturbation of spirit, bringing as interpreter one of the English residents. Talking with great rapidity, his fez very much on one side, his face the picture of woe, he confided ghastly fears for his life. Speedily translated into English, the burden of his tale appeared that the husbands of all the ladies who were guests at his wedding festivities had each taken an alarm lest his particular wives might have been photographed when I turned the camera on the various balconies and groups.

"And now they lie in wait for me at every corner," he continued, his face pale and drawn. "There will be feuds and family disturbances for generations, and *bloodshed*," he went on excitedly. "They will have my life!"

"That is certainly unpleasant," I said, "and embarrassing for you; but why should they take my innocent little camera so seriously?"

"Ah, but a *man* might develop the nega-

tives," he replied, " and so see their faces —
or you might show them when you get home
(is it so far?); or some — some man (a Christian!) might see those faces. And they will
not forgive that it was in my house these fatali-
ties occurred." And the poor fellow, who had
a fine, open face, almost wrung his hands in
the extremity of his distress.

Seeing that it behooved me if possible to
rescue him from all his horrors, I told him he
might have the films from the camera, just as
they were, undeveloped. Then there could be
no danger of my carrying away forbidden faces
to any lands where they might be looked upon
by the unregenerate.

He beamed with joy, pocketed them radi-
antly, and with a thousand thanks bowed himself out into the waiting retributions of the
night, now shorn of their powers.

The eager development of the film revealed
no record.

Sudanese hut

XVI

Wedding Preliminaries

The early days of a wedding week were full of strange interest.

On Monday festivities usually began at the bride's home. On arrival we found a great assemblage of very resplendent ladies in yards of gold coins and necklaces, incredibly heavy earrings, bracelets to the elbow of the usual soft, thick gold; silver and gold gauze, and blue, green, crimson or yellow silk; violently painted faces, sleeveless jackets of royal purple or wine-coloured velvet, embroidered thickly in gold, with silk barracans lightly draped. Here and there were other brown Bedouins, fascinating creatures with short, strong white teeth, red handkerchiefs tied coquettishly over their black hair, pounds of silver clasps and chains, earrings and bracelets; bare feet and open, trustful faces.

TRIPOLI THE MYSTERIOUS

Some of the ladies were tightly wrapped in thin white barracans, hardly the one allowable eye exposed. They stood timidly together, most careful not to let their faces be seen even for an instant, though none but women were present. Certain husbands in Tripoli were known as especially opposed to their wives ever venturing out of the home, even tightly swathed, and were they recognized here, some mischief-making person might report their probably surreptitious presence. It was whispered that one or two would probably then receive a beating. On this occasion we were invited to the gallery and looked down upon the brilliantly decked assembly.

After a time the door of the bride's room opposite was quietly, cautiously opened, the negro women who always supply music on these occasions gathering around it, with much chanting and beating on drums, and with them a little girl carrying a lovely old silver lamp in which incense was burning. First to emerge were women bearing a fine rectangular cushion of crimson velvet embroidered in gold. Others followed with a bushel basket full of dried henna leaves. All went carefully down the stairway with their burdens into the open court-yard below, placing the henna on the central cushion.

A huge black Sudanese servant came next, carrying with greatest care an immense mir-ror in a gilt frame. Supported and guided on either hand by gorgeous females came the shrouded figure of the bride, gracefully wrapped in a cloth-of-gold barracan, brought around to a point on top of her head, the two sides evidently basted together, completely to cover the face. Her crimson velvet slippers were embroidered in gold, and she stepped slowly and cautiously, both as befitted a tem-porarily blinded lady, and one occupying for the time so exalted a position. As close as possible to the mirror she was kept, facing it all the way around the gallery, still accom-panied by the guiding friend and incense bearer, then, with some difficulty, down the stairs. All this occupied nearly half an hour. Once below, she walked impressively to the middle of the courtyard, where the mirror was held close to the cushion and its basket. Stepping between, she seated herself in the basket facing the mirror, her attendants adjusting the barracan for her greater comfort, and, once seated, jumping her gently up and down on the yielding leaves. The henna was picked up in handfuls by her friends, passed over her, given into her hands under her draperies, and put entirely over and about her. Pressing her face close to the mirror, she opened the barracan to gaze at herself, while her friends spread their own draperies out as a shield, that by no chance could a glimpse of her face be caught from any angle. This part of the ceremony savoured greatly of mystery, and was evidently symbolic. No Mohammedan woman with whom I talked, no matter how friendly or how long the acquaintance, was ever willing to explain this performance. All seemed to regard it as too sacred for discussion, and always changed the subject if I broached it, although ever ready to talk upon all other aspects of these occasions.

Finally the big black picked up the mirror once more, and began his return march upward, bride and attendants following; cushion and basket were removed, and the company dispersed. The bride retreated to her own room, and the door was fastened, her friends not being supposed to see her again until evening, when the more intimate would take supper with her, in the closed room. But as we were strangers, and soon leaving, we were invited in then and there. The bride was seated on the floor, five or six especial friends about, her beautiful barracan off, and wearing a pretty dress of simple red and white cotton. She was an especially attractive girl, bright and wholesome, with an expression of humour and strength rare in Tripoli.

A fortunate man, her husband to be, who had not yet seen his new wife!

XVII

Another Mohammedan Wedding

For two or three nights we had been again aroused by weird processions, and the day following the third, a closely veiled native woman came to escort us to another " sitting out " of a bride. It was at a house in an entirely unfamiliar part of the city. The streets were narrower, and not a foreigner was seen, as we rapidly approached the festive courtyard. It was absolutely packed with humanity when we arrived, so that we were invited to the gallery, as a better view-point.

Flocks of exquisite white pigeons were flying in and out everywhere, swooping down from the blue above, crossing the housetop, almost alighting, and then — off again in the sunshine. Looped across one corner of the gallery were strings of dreadful meat, several

108

pieces of which had been thrown on the floor for a cat, whose possession of the dainties was being vigorously disputed by a creeping baby not more than six or seven months old.

All the guests were of course very gayly arrayed, a few as before keeping themselves tightly shrouded, as if they had secretly stolen out of their own harems and feared recognition. One or two handsome Turkish women were present, some well-dressed blacks, and again a few splendidly picturesque Bedouins in magnificent silver. One of these old women seemed to possess a veritable gift of humour; she showed her strong white teeth in many hearty laughs, her red turban was set rakishly on one side, her long veil caught by a fine filigree silver disk, and her fingers were deeply henna-dyed.

As usual, black women sat upon the courtyard floor, beating strange drums and chanting in peculiar rhythm, one of them becoming to all appearance absolutely intoxicated with her own performance, her four straight, spiked,

109

jessamine blossoms vibrating over one ear, the whole body swaying in joyous unison to the tempo of her barbaric song.

Several women had brought babies, some of whom appeared fairly healthy and strong, but more were very pale and indifferent. Babies in Tripoli were supposed to eat anything handy — meat, yellow bread from the street, fruit, or whatever their parents enjoyed; and if a woman could not nurse her baby its chances for life were very slight. Infant mortality was appalling. One tiny mite was evidently dying on the spot; not a particle of flesh on its wee arms and legs, on which the skin hung in folds. It was perfectly white, and breathing with difficulty, yet its mother was dandling it, trying to amuse its closing eyes, and pretending to herself that it was like other little babies.

Near us on the gallery was a carefully guarded door of pale green, with handsome drop handles of brass, watched by a stout and ancient grandmother of the bride (rather care-

ANOTHER MOHAMMEDAN WEDDING

less of her barracan), who held it shut as final stages of the bridal toilet went on.

Half a dozen intimate friends now entered to view the heroine, then a few more, then the black women with tambourines to escort her down, and four little girls with tiny lighted candles. On the way a small boy disputed candle-bearing rights, and sent one little girl off in bitter tears, while he triumphantly joined the procession in her place.

This bride was enfolded in a blue striped silk veil, nearly covering very long braids of black hair with heavy silver ornaments at the ends, her dress chiefly wine-coloured velvet and blue velvet, gold embroidered and silver embroidered, and silver slippers. She was led downward most tenderly, as if she might have been spun glass. A bride is treated with much honour in her husband's house for a month, his mother and all the family vying with each other to relieve her from care and labour. After that she takes her place with the rest, doing even more than her normal share.

TRIPOLI THE MYSTERIOUS

At last in the courtyard, the present heroine was put up on a green chest ornamented with brass, evidently containing her treasures; hands and draperies were adjusted, and then she was turned solemnly around like a lay figure, that all might view her deeply henna-dyed fingers with their gold-leaf ornaments, her fine clothes and jewelry. The veil finally put back, a densely powdered and pink-tri-angled face emerged, blackened eyebrows meeting, gilt and coloured paper adornments pasted on chin and forehead, chains of blossoms and all the rest, familiar from the earlier wedding. It was about at this point that we had arrived on the scene of the former ceremony; for now, having turned this bride around quite sufficiently to have produced genuine vertigo, she was gently led off her box and it was carried out. She was placed in a chair against the wall, veil pinned up to fall in folds behind, her hands were spread on her knees, and every one pressed up to examine her costume.

There she would sit until dark.

XVIII

A Jewish–Arab Wedding

An Arab wedding among wealthy Jews is differently conducted.

Invitations had reached us several days before, and were accepted with vivid interest. The house was a fine one, yet as usual, even with the most prosperous families, situated in a mean and narrow street, approached through what looked like a subterranean passage, winding and full of turns and corners, in the Harah quarter of the city.

We finally reached the courtyard, open to the sky, and guarded by servants at the entrance. Even the walls of the passages leading in were covered by enormously long leaves of the date palm, also the pale-blue walls of the courtyard itself. Woven silk hangings were draped in a variety of ways, with bright silk veils and large handkerchiefs.

Immediately facing the entrance was a raised platform, upon it a sofa and easy-chairs faced each other on either side, making a sort of throne, with fine white barracans of camel's hair and silk. In the center, suspended from cross-beams, was a large, openwork ornament covered with artificial roses, gilt balls and other tinsel. On the undraped sofa were an embroidered bag and a Tripoli fan like a little flag, only not made this time of straw, but jessamine blossoms on wire. The floor and daïs were covered with very good rugs.

Above, the gallery was filled with friends, and the roof as well—evidently neighbours had crept along above, and were staring down on the gay scene uninvited. Jewish ladies were collecting in leisurely style, dressed in every imaginable colour, but the effect softened and poeticized by their lovely barracans which when draped allowed only faces, the front of their hair and enormous earrings and necklaces to be seen. A very few Maltese and Italians came in European dress, but not enough to spoil the oriental effect. Handsome young Jewish men in fezzes, long broadcloth coats and white shirts flapping outside the large trousers, handed chairs, looked after the guests, and were exceedingly thoughtful and attentive.

More and more guests kept arriving, many with children, and the rooms off the courtyard were filled, every grating and window aglow with gazing eyes.

The father and mother of the bride, with strong, sweet faces, passed about among their friends, he in fez and round blue turban, she in braided hair, much jewelry and many colours. They and their oldest son together boasted eighteen children. The son was very handsome.

Finally we became conscious of Turkish singing by people hidden from sight, two or three notes, nasal beyond belief, continued iteration, no beginning or ending, no melody, no tonic, no seventh, and very loud.

Shortly after, two dignified rabbis in robes

and turbans came down the open stairway from the gallery, one very round and fat, the other phenomenally tall and slender, followed by two little girls carrying enormous lighted candles. The mother of the bride and mother of the groom followed, and then the bridal pair. The little bride was plump and pretty, with long, curling black lashes, many colours in jackets and skirts and trousers, and over all a white tulle veil. The groom was a sallow and unhandsome boy.

They mounted the little platform, she at his right in seating themselves on the sofa. He at once drew over their heads a silk scarf, quite wide, of white with lavender ends. It was soon dropped off, and they sat still, her eyes demurely cast down; her mother occupied the arm-chair next the groom, his next the bride.

One of the rabbis then took a glass of wine, saying a long invocation of some kind over it, drinking a little himself and sending it afterward to the bridegroom, who put it to his bride's lips (and spilled a lot down her neck, poor boy!). The same goblet was passed around among the guests, each taking a sip. Then more sonorous words repeated by the rabbi, many responses in unison by the company, the flash of a wedding ring which presumably reached the bride, her veil was lifted — and suddenly glasses of something flavoured with rose water were being passed about, huge blocks of sponge cake, and dessert-spoonfuls of candies, some of bright blue.

Very soon all the women guests began to press about the bride, kissing both her cheeks and shaking hands. Finally we went to her and paid our respects, also to the bridegroom's mother and that of the bride, this time our real hostess.

On emerging into the cavernous white street, it was still bright daylight, with deep-blue sky blazing in a narrow ribbon above white walls and intermittent masonry arches of pale yellow, pink, lavender and blue. Camels were claiming right of way, and patient donkeys,

TRIPOLI THE MYSTERIOUS

proud Turks, veiled women, lordly Jews, sober Arabs passed swiftly like theatrical setting.

Was it indeed our own world at all — or not, rather, some sudden plunge into the life of a new planet?

All the instruments were in readiness on the Consulate roof-terrace

XIX

THE ECLIPSE OF 1900

All the instruments were in readiness on the Consulate roof-terrace. All the amateur helpers in various lines of observation — those to draw the corona, to mark time, to watch for and record Baily's Beads, shadow-bands and various minor phenomena — had been carefully drilled, and the time was nearly at hand.

As the day approached, skies seemed to grow constantly clearer. In the dry season no storms were, of course, to be apprehended, yet this did not mean entire immunity from cloud, and the *gibleh* might start up, thickening the air dangerously for photographing fine filaments of the corona. On that fateful Monday morning, however, I awoke from frightful dreams of fog and storm to find a crystal morning with atmosphere of unsurpassed and limpid purity.

TRIPOLI THE MYSTERIOUS

Every suggestion of wandering vapour about the horizon disappeared as the morning advanced, and the sky became absolutely transparent. In intervals of giving final instructions to workmen and voluntary observers of all nations, and helping here and there, above and below, I kept a wary eye on the sky, but always found it the same tender blue, unstained. Finally the afternoon came, every one had gathered, rehearsals of the past six days were once more repeated, and the entire English colony with a few French and Italians were placed, each at an appointed spot to perform his part in the eclipse programme.

The glare of white roofs was almost blinding, the arrogant sun unconscious of his approaching humiliation shining with intensified brilliance, as if to compel human retreat from the terrace.

More than two hours before the eclipse reached us, came a telegram from Georgia, announcing the success of observations there —a veritable triumph of man's messenger

A telegram from Georgia

over the speed of heavenly bodies, the possibility of which had been already demonstrated by Professor Todd in January, 1889, during the California eclipse. In just twenty-nine minutes after the Georgia observations were made, in fourteen from Washington, came the prearranged cipher describing the eclipse at the American end of its track.

On my husband's application and by the courtesy of Denison Pender, Esq., General Manager of the extensive lines of the Eastern Telegraph Company, use of their new cables from Gibraltar to Malta and from Malta to Tripoli was granted, enabling this very rapid communication, and the complete worsting of the moon in its race with electricity.

The Italian drawing-master and a few of his best pupils were gathered at one corner, plumb-lines before them to indicate the direction of coronal rays in their sketches; near by, the roof had been marked with north and south lines to show direction and speed of shadow-bands, with observers stationed at

121

hand; a camera was turned upon that part of the white wall where the shadow of the great tree would fall, that possibly the tiny crescents revealed by its foliage during the partial eclipse might be caught upon the plate; two or three disks were set up, with observers behind them, to cut off the bright light of the inner corona; thus the long extensions might be more easily seen and depicted. Small telescopes to be used visually upon sections of the corona were placed at various points, persons to watch the approach of the moon's shadow and its recession — all were expectant, waiting; while the real work and effort were concentrated at the ten telescopes and their clockwork, already turned upon that spot in the sky where the sun would be at totality.

Every roof all over the city was swarming with humanity, Maltese, Jews, Arabs, Turkish soldiers on their upper ramparts, Franciscan monks on their high-air promenade — even the minarets were crowded, while in the streets

The tiny crescents revealed by its foliage during the partial eclipse.

below a curious crowd collected, craning the universal neck to catch, perchance, a glimpse of the telescopes and the favoured few on the Consulate roof. Whatever " show " was coming must be there, and to get a sight of us was the great thing. Only one man in the city seemed totally oblivious of a spectacle impending, and he, wrapped up in his *cashabiya,* continued to shake barley in a sieve stupidly, far below in a shaded courtyard.

About quarter after four first contact was observed, a bit ahead of time. The faithful moon had crept on and on toward the great moment when she should glide in between us and the sun, and with her small bulk offer the only screen to his brilliancy which has ever been effective in allowing a sight of the corona to mortal eyes. The first " bite " into his dazzling disk had been taken, and silently on-creeping, the sun's extinguisher covered more and more of the shining surface until only a stout crescent remained. Even then the light seemed hardly less, the glare of white roofs was still painful to unshaded eyes, but there was a slightly different tone in the sunshine.

A few moments later it was no longer uncomfortable to gaze abroad, the colour of everything visible was sad, subdued; the sapphire sea became a cold slate, the sky like steel. A few cries ascended from below as the weird quality in the light grew more insistent and the muezzins' prayer call arose, but in general a singular silence prevailed. It became cool and damp, and the swallows emerged in flocks, flying about excitedly in a manner quite unlike their nightly sunset parade. Camels dropped upon their knees, and other animals exhibited much uneasiness.

Suddenly the tiny crescent, scarcely more than a thread, shortened from both cusps simultaneously, and all the bright line broke up into a series of globules or drops, called Baily's Beads, first mentioned by Halley in 1715, a dainty and beautiful phenomenon.

Totality was upon us. It came, not with a majestic leap as at Esashi in 1896, nor in a series of jerks, the effect at Shirakawa in 1887, but in a silent unfolding, inexpressibly majestic and lovely. One second the luminous drops, as the shining crescent broke up — the next, there hung the great black ball of the moon in the clear, gray-purple sky, while around it blossomed the exquisite corona, like some fair flower of celestial light. Two long streamers below, the upper edge of one brilliantly shining, the rest soft and silvery, with three equally extended rays above, of interwoven structure and brightly white points, the polar rays short and inconspicuous — this corona glowed in elusive fairy-like beauty above the dreaming desert, while planets emerged in the cool sky, and a hush as of eternal waiting pervaded the still air.

Low on the horizon a warm yellow breathed along the shore, but there was none of the majesty of colour, the unearthly effect of a new creation, which made the Esashi eclipse so heart-breakingly superb, so thrilling, so breathless. Instead, this was normal, tender, lovely, full of masterful beauty and power, yet with a peace breathing the very spirit of interplanetary space, where time is not, where nothing is old, yet never young, in presence of which mere human emotion fades and faints and utterly dies away. The great psychic currents of the universe, in their moral and spiritual onrush and splendid vitality, never flow with such an overwhelming, tangible rush as in these moments of cosmic silence, of repressed, superb possibility.

I looked for twenty seconds — and never did they flee with such amazing speed — and for thirty more I sketched the streamers with prosaic pencil and paper. It was like attempting to catch the solar system in a bird-cage.

A needle-shaft of true, returning sunlight flashed over the world, and again that strange, invariable sigh from the hushed multitude, as of tension relaxed, rose from the streets like a veritable tribute to immensity. Totality was over.

But gravity all the time had been doing its

work, and more than a hundred exposures
made during those fifty seconds, the whole
mechanism so perfectly planned that as the
fiftieth second closed, the sand weights just
touched the courtyard pavement below; and on
each plate a clear picture of the corona without the touch of a human hand, except to re-
lease the pin at the beginning for the mechanism to operate. The other telescopes had also
made their record; and a fruitful harvest of
amateur sketches was garnered.

All the natives insisted that totality was preceded by "a thick smoke," undoubtedly the
moon's onrushing shadow over the white city.
But it is contrary to their religion to investigate
the workings of nature, so that when questioned
about the eclipse they would not make any detailed comments upon what they saw. They
have a curious fear of extolling the creature
above the Creator, and in general all they
would say was "Allah is Almighty," "His
works are wonderful," and other indis-
putable propositions of a similar nature. A

very few, only, ventured to talk of what they saw, and that without betraying any sentiment of admiration or wonder.

Beautiful, brief totality! Its tantalizing hint of solar secrets made more definite the plan of attack for another eclipse.

XX

The Pianura Market

The Tuesday market, Suk el-Thalath, is held in a huge open space beyond the city, along the wide beach. Almost an epitome of the city's varied life, products of native industry appear in primitive guise. On the outskirts are crowded animals for sale, regiments of camels, here and there a white one or a baby camel, goats in great flocks, kids, little cows, sheep, donkeys, ponies; and bales of esparto grass, through which comes a large part of the actual income of the city. It grows wild on the hilly boundary between barren dunes and arable oases, generally indicating absence of other vegetation. Loads of two hundred weight each are brought in large nets, the camels quite concealed by their verdant burden.

The tiny tents arose in a night, a weekly no-

129

madic city in street after street, one devoted
to vendors of meat, product of unfamiliar animals in unknown shapes; curious vegetables
occupied the attention of one tent-lane, with
apricots and mulberries; another street showed
coral, roughly shaped to native uses; near by,
sponges, gathered close at hand by Greek
fishermen; one was exclusively occupied by
the boys and women who make straw covers,
oddly woven with bits of gayly coloured cloth,
as protection to the precious *cus-cus* from dust
or insects; still another miniature highway
showed only coarse cotton bonnets for babies,
ornamented with bright wool in varying designs. One old woman selling a sort of ban-
dana handkerchief had large cylinders of red
coral stuck through each nostril.

Smooth-haired goats were led about by a
horn or an ear, tiny cows were urged hither
and yon, and people, goods, animals were so
closely packed that movement was almost
impossible.

Upon the wide white beach no less than ten

An anxious mother

Straw covers . . . protection to the precious *cus-cus*

thousand natives would assemble for this
Tuesday sale and barter. Bedouins, proud and
silent, frequently prosperous, yet spending less
for daily living than the poorest European
labourer, stalked about, inspecting bargains.
No wares were there to attract moneyed
strangers, only things the native wants and
will buy; no attempts at English to flatter the
passing purchaser, but only the motley residents were considered — even the lordly Arab
in white deigning to supply himself here, and
proceeding homeward to some far oasis of the
desert, sometimes on a blooded horse covered
with gay leather and brass and silver trap-
pings, his draperies eddying in the wind, and
ten feet of gun protruding; frequently sitting
far back on his patient donkey laden as well
with family necessities for a week to come.

With all its polyglot life of caravan and sil-
versmith, wine merchant and ivory seller, camel
market and carpet bazar, these hot Tuesday
mornings on the sands seem sometimes in
retrospect the very spirit of the white city's

singular charm. The iridescent Mediterranean, breaking in gentlest ripples against a
shining beach, white walls and domes and
castle in the distance, and close at hand camels
and horses, baskets and rugs, coral and silver,
and the surging life of thousands — shrouded
Arabs, uncovered blacks and befezzed Turks
— all this was Tripoli in essence, under the
burning blue of an African sky.

An intensely picturesque black man surrounded by a wild group of Fezzani was holding them enthralled by his tales, until their
grasping hands relaxed, their purchases fell to
the sand, and they literally hung upon his
words in breathless tension. A few rods farther on, an ancient negress with ears and nose
stuck full of bars of red coral, and fuzzy wool
to match, seated flat on the beach, was holding
forth similarly to an enchained audience. Her
voice carried me miles out into the desert. I
heard the winds of great Sahara play about
my head and the elemental spirit of space utter
its unapprehended wisdom.

Camel laden with esparto grass

By noon the crowd disperses

THE PIANURA MARKET

The prevalence of fiery red wool among negresses was somewhat surprising, and its explanation rather more so. Nothing, it seems is so much dreaded by these simple women as the appearance of white streaks among the black, and at the first shadowy suggestion of approaching grayness immediate resort is had to the dyepot, a brilliant vermilion, seemingly, the only available tint. Hence the frequent but strangely amusing combination, the startling effect, of ebony faces surmounted by orange-scarlet wool.

By noon the crowd disperses, and the open beach is left once more to its normal white smoothness; tents are gone, animals have trotted away, nationalities are scattered, and one of the most picturesque events in the life of Tripoli is over for a week.

XXI

Bread Market and Caravans

For many years Tripoli had almost a monopoly of the caravan trade. The city is the Mediterranean Mecca for long lines of camels streaming in from depths of desert spaces, bringing ivory and gold dust, ostrich feathers and gums, wax and tanned leather, sometimes mats and henna, and using three or four months or longer for their deliberate progress. Returning probably before the year is out, here begin the principal routes of commerce from Barbary to the far interior oases, carrying in exchange Manchester prints, tea and sugar. Fanatical Tuaregs, their faces shrouded in veils as well as barracan, closed palanquins on the best camels for the concealment of accompanying (supposable) beauty, and barbarous musicians of the desert, made a strange pro-

134

Bread market

cession, often taking hours for entire arrival after the leading dromedaries had appeared.

The Tuaregs have never been conquered. Fully twenty thousand in number, no treachery or cruelty seems too great for them to inflict upon foreigners of the hated Christian belief unhappy enough to get into their power. Yet, besides their abnormally long guns, many members of the caravans I watched, even Tuaregs themselves, carried Crusader swords, with the cross for a handle, and many swarthy girls of certain tribes had small blue-black crosses tattooed between the eyebrows, a racial mark far removed from its original significance and all unthought of by these loyal adherents of the prophet.

Caravans for the Sudan take either the Fezzan or the Ghadames route, practically the same as far as the oasis of Misda, south of the Gharian mountains, where the caravans sometimes halt in their long march. Fezzan is an archipelago of oases, those islands of the desert. Warmer than Tripoli in climate, it is supposed to have about one hundred thousand inhabitants. Like other North African regions, the camel is the chief domestic animal, but a few foxes, gazelles and antelopes are kept.

Fanaticism, greed and intolerance have kept Europeans out of the oasis of Ghat; Moslems only are allowed there. It is the gateway to the western Sahara of Tripoli.

In Zellah and Tirsa ostriches are raised. Beyond this point those bound for the western Sudan follow the southwest route to Ghadames; and to Bornu Kuka or the places on Lake Tchad by the southeast route, far more difficult. The way for those starting from Benghazi is considered very dangerous for Europeans. But Tripoli seems the natural connecting link between Europe and Africa. In past years European merchandise was stored here until time for a caravan to set out for the Sudan, and African goods also waited here for transportation across the Mediterranean.

BREAD MARKET AND CARAVANS

Commerce with the interior was constant, and ostrich feathers, elephant tusks, skins, even gold, came up in quantities by caravan from Bornu and Uadai, in exchange for Manchester cloths, Venetian glass-ware, and goods from southern France. Prosperous merchants, sending off wares into desert depths, heard nothing for months, sometimes for years, of their fate. Frequently all hope was abandoned, but when a returning caravan was actually sighted, camels slow and weary, men hungry, thirsty, sunburned, all Tripoli went out to the city gates, and the train was met with such rejoicing welcome as is rarely accorded home-coming wanderers in more civilized regions. Five hundred or even a thousand camels used to be dispatched. Now, although Tripoli is still the point of departure for such expeditions, they are smaller and far more infrequent.

One of the picturesque quarters of the city is the square which on certain days is used as the bread market, where hundreds of Arabs crouch all day under their barracans in the

137

hot sunshine, keeping guard over loaves of bright yellow and other tints, unhygienic but artistic. The scene was always quaint and alluring. Near by in a shaded corner the white caps worn under the fez were sold, and men and animals filled the open spaces with a tumultuous yet strangely silent life.

To me this bread market will always be associated with one memorable morning. For the first time in many months a caravan had been sighted, and was even then beginning to arrive, after ten months' weary crossing of the well-nigh limitless desert. The camels stepped slowly, heavily laden with huge bales securely tied up — ivory and gold dust, skins and feathers. On the saddles were gay rugs and blankets, a few good saddle-bags, but generally uninteresting in pattern and quality. Wrapped in dingy drapery and carrying guns ten feet long, swarthy Bedouins led the weary camels across the sun-baked square. In the singular and silent company marched a few genuine Tuaregs, black veils strapped tightly

138

Word came . . . that about three hundred men and camels were just ready for departure

over their faces, and enshrouded in black or dark brown wraps, unlike the barracan. In their opinion even the veils were hardly protection against the impious glances of hated Christians, and with attitudes expressive of the utmost repulsion and ferocity they turned aside, lest a glance might be met in passing. All were ragged beyond belief and incredibly dirty.

Over two hundred and fifty camels composed the train, one or two carrying tightly closed palanquins in which favorite wives rode in safe retirement. Arabs, Bedouins, Tuaregs even, looked worn and tired; and far out into the desert stretched the incoming horde.

Once only during our months in Tripoli an important caravan set forth from the city for the far south. Word came one day during luncheon that about three hundred men and camels were just ready for departure. Hastening to the famous " three palms " from which the start was made, we found a scene of great activity. Numerous camels, already loaded, were hobbled and waiting for the start. Bales still covered the ground, and many animals were kneeling to receive their burdens. The leader, a racing camel, with high Tuareg saddle, watched us intelligently with an expression of alert though impersonal interest. I took a few pictures, manifestly an operation not very pleasing to the busy Arabs, and for several hours we remained in the vicinity, fascinated by the strange scene.

Toward five, though all was not yet in readiness, forty or fifty camels and their masters set out slowly from the city for the first short stage of their immense journey. Camp would be made that night near by, where all late comers would join the main body; and next day, a unit, the train would leave comforts behind for weary months.

140

Bales still covered the ground

The leader, a racing camel with high Tuareg saddle

XXII

Music and Musicians

A strange, hypnotic quality characterized the native music of Tripoli. Various crude instruments were used, goatskins in the hands of Sudanese, strange flageolets, cymbals, stringed instruments; the street singing, story telling and weird chants performed by black women at Arab weddings, all had some peculiar effect very hard to analyze. The death dirge rising from a near-by courtyard throughout a whole night carried a wail of despair from which no escape seemed possible. The Turkish military band discoursed most amazing music, always ending with a blessing on the Sultan in unison. But this was merely interesting, not terrifying.

Sometimes at dawn, when roofs and minarets were dazzlingly white against the sap-

phire sky, already shining in affluent sunlight
while yet the labyrinthine streets at the bot-
tom of stucco cañons lay in twilight gray,
strange men from the desert would stalk by,
making uncanny music. One of them, very
tall and blacker than most, was dressed in a
low-necked, short-sleeved garment, greatly ab-
breviated as to skirts; playing melodies in a
minor mode unknown to the West, his stride
was full of a dignity well-nigh appalling.
Once or twice I tried to write these melodies
in our own familiar notation, but it would have
been as easy to transcribe the wind or surf-beat
on the sand. The instrument slightly re-
sembled a Scotch bagpipe, decorated with barbaric strings of shells and beads — an inflated
skin with primitive mouthpiece, and at the opposite end two pointed projections like horns.
These he held in either hand, and might almost
have passed for the Japanese god of winds,
blowing alternately, as the freak took him,
typhoons and hurricanes, or zephyrs only
strong enough to waft cherry-blossom petals

An inflated skin with primitive mouthpiece

from the bough; except that no element of the humourous crossed the stern, implacable face of this son of the desert, high with lofty thought of gods and fates. His companion beat upon a curious little tom-tom, now and then singing a blood-curdling chant. This was hardly easier to transcribe into familiar notation than the mournful bag-pipe, yet the rhythm was marked and unchanging, and as nearly as notes can express it, the following: —

Distinctly major, yet it joined harmoniously
with the moan of the instrument, quite as
definitely not major.

Black boys following, jumped, shouted,
danced like wild creatures, excited beyond all
bounds by this oddly compelling music, as the
rhythm penetrated and seized their imagination.
Generally passing about sunrise, these men of
mystery sometimes went by in the night, the
weird performance once or twice taking place
about two o'clock in the morning. The min-
strels always walked with peculiar swiftness,
intent upon the serious business in hand. Lis-
tening for long to the mystic strains, a singular
influence was discernible. One had actually to
exercise distinct self-control not to follow after
these enticing sounds, whithersoever they
might beckon.

Hardly less insistent was an old woman who
played upon a *gimbei*, like an undeveloped
banjo, and sang in a high and cracked but tireless voice words apparently fraught with dis-
astrous meaning, bringing to mind grewsome

Taking her station against some white wall

stories of desert depths. Taking her station against some white wall, prickly pears high above her head against the blue, she chanted for hours, surrounded by a fascinated audience gradually augmenting as her climaxes approached. One of the favourite African professions, apparently, this intoning stories to a circle of listeners.

There is more in it than mere sound. I have been myself transported bodily into the depths of Sahara by these monotonously chanted tales. I have felt the free winds blow in my face as the racing dromedary bore me on to strange scenes over moonlit sands.

XXIII

TURKISH EXILES AND OTHERS

Redjed Pasha, Governor of Tripoli, a gentleman of much intelligence, was deeply interested in the coming eclipse, and even offered his castle, once the ancient citadel, as site for telescopes and cameras, and headquarters for the expedition. Frequently he called upon us at the Consulate, inspecting progress in mounting apparatus, and expressing his certainty that Allah would grant clear skies on the important day. The Pasha's nearest officers were socially delightful men of the world, thoroughly cultivated, speaking several languages, who made our stay memorable in various thoughtful ways.

On our earlier visit his official call was made with his retinue and much gold and glory on May 24, the Queen's birthday.

The Pasha confessed that he was deeply curious about the telescopes

TURKISH EXILES AND OTHERS

In 1905 his first call was also made in state.
All the gorgeous cavasses were double lined
to receive him, the British flag was hoisted
and the Consul-General and the Astronomer
met him on the gallery. Three resplendent
officers accompanied him, in red fezzes and
perfect European dress. After refreshments
and necessary compliments, the Pasha confessed that he was deeply curious about the
telescopes and the way the Astronomer was
planning to observe the eclipse. Then with his
retinue he proceeded to the roof-terrace where
our own little American flag was flying, and
examined thoroughly all the apparatus. He
said it would please him if we would photograph him and his officers with the Astronomer,
which was gladly done.

The good Pasha quite took us under his
protection. People stood up against walls to
see us go by, day after day, in charge of
one imperial officer after another and in
different carriages; once or twice with
three white horses abreast, which could

barely make their way through the crowded thoroughfares.

As Tripoli was a sort of colony for political suspects, a good many exiles lived in the white city who brought the very atmosphere of Constantinople with them, the elegance, the grace of living which no transportation could disguise. One of these was F—— Bey, a handsome young man near to the Pasha in the castle, of great wealth and high family, who was still trying to find out why he was exiled. Unconscious of having thought or said, much less done, anything disloyal to the Sultan, he unexpectedly and very suddenly found himself in Tripoli, forbidden to return " for the present." He had sent for his mother and sister, elegant women of rank, in whose society, at their secluded but richly appointed home, we found the greatest pleasure. This, however, was before the " Young Turk " movement and during the reign of Abdul Hamid II. The recall of our friend to his former haunts followed the coming of more liberal ideas.

148

One of these . . . was still trying to find
out why he was exiled

TURKISH EXILES AND OTHERS

Many other interesting exiles were banished from Constantinople for they knew not what imaginary offense or suspected crime, but their loyalty to the Sultan seemed unshaken, their almost daily hope of return pathetically unquenched.

Old Etim Bey especially, speaking only Turkish, debarred from returning because he "knew too much," became a warm friend, inviting us constantly to his chaotic house, full of curios, photographs, musical instruments, guns, pistols, cameras, inventions from the world over — even an automobile which would not go, and could not have been navigated in Tripoli's uncertain streets had it ever so good a will to go.

Learned Jewish rabbis speaking and writing only Hebrew called frequently, telling many a tale of intense interest and significance of the region and its history.

In the roadstead lay always several men of war, Italian, French, English, among them an old Turkish craft supposed hardly seaworthy enough to get out of harbour if escape were necessary, but upon whose ample decks delightful hospitality was dispensed by her officers.

The first foreign lady to be invited on board, I felt the honour of that position when the chief officer and the Captain of the Port came for us in the launch. Rowed by stout Turkish arms, we rapidly approached the old wooden cruiser, the star and crescent ensign floating proudly at our stern. The Commander met us at the gangway, the crew all standing at attention as we came on board; and coffee, sweetmeats and cigarettes were served at once on the clean and breezy afterdeck. More substantial refreshments were offered later in the Commander's airy cabin. The ship's guns, probably fiercer in appearance than in action, added much to the decorative effect.

A Greek warship, the *Crete*, modern in every appointment, looking particularly after the sponge-divers and their interests, brought a number of extremely intelligent and agreeable young officers, who entertained on board

. . . his chaotic house full of curios

with much elegance, and gave valuable assistance in our eclipse observations.

Nothing mediæval or rusty characterized the
Crete; she was a fine, clean, up-to-date naval
vessel. Delicious luncheons were served;
among other sweetmeats was a Greek fig
paste, quite different from the Turkish *rah
hat lu cum,* yet somewhat similar in flavour.

The Consul-General of Great Britain and
the Vice-Consul, the head of the cable service,
one or two gentlemen in business and in charge
of the export to England of feathers, ivory
or esparto grass, an English medical mis-
sionary who was a trained engineer, the
French and Italian Consuls — these friends
with their families brought every curious and
valuable aspect of the region to our attention,
showed us how to utilize times and seasons
to the best advantage, and out of the experience of long residence gave untold assistance
in our study of all these strange surroundings.

Many dinner-parties I remember on galleries
overlooking beautiful courtyards where shaded

lights gleamed through palm and vine, the delicious drip of falling fountains filled the warm air, and soft-footed, white-robed Arab servants appeared and disappeared with the certainty and timeliness of a happy fate.

The city did remain quiescent in the sense of world progress, but its charm, untranslatable yet potent, was never to be resisted.

From any roof terrace in Tripoli a dozen minarets . . . could be seen

XXIV

Mosques

From any roof terrace in Tripoli a dozen
minarets and countless domes could be seen.
The beautiful white city of Barbary was
Mohammedan to the core, fanatical, sober,
dignified. Five times a day, as faithfully as
in Constantinople itself, shrouded muezzins
emerged upon their lofty towers, calling the
faithful to prayer in varying melodies of two
or three notes invariably founded upon the
harmonic minor scale, the seventh frequently
omitted — a peculiarity of many less civilized
races. Occasionally, as if by accident, a major
third sounded with unexpected effect. The
quality of tone is singularly penetrating, but
generally unmusical. Melodies were varied,
one being almost a chant in impressive solem-

nity, while another was always several times re-

peated. Unfailingly a third muezzin reiterated

Until our advent the mosques, unlike those
of Algiers, had never been profaned by infidel
footsteps. They were closed tightly against
Christians. Through an ornate green doorway
opposite the Roman arch, where constantly sat
a melancholy leper awaiting possible alms, I
had often caught glimpses, past entering worshipers, of a dark but lovely interior, with the
faint, characteristic tinkle of running water.
Not, however, until we had spent several weeks
in the city was sufficient influence brought to
bear to admit us to the sacred precincts, and
then we were conducted by the head dragoman
of the British Consulate, *cavasse* and interpreter, an imposing yet kindly Arab, and one
of the mosque's most dignified officers. A truly
royal man in appearance, he was often most

Where constantly sat a melancholy leper awaiting possible alms

gorgeously arrayed. On the queen's birthday in 1900, when Turkish officials paid their calls of state upon Her Majesty's representative, Mufta was resplendent in yellow brocade and gold with white silk barracan. Later in the day he wore a scarlet, gold-embroidered uniform. But on the occasion when we accompanied him to his great, seventeen-domed mosque, he was covered only by the plain barracan of devotion.

Within the forbidden sanctuary, I first noticed two enormous Turkey carpets, a hundred years old, covering the floor, except a narrow space between, where a number of worshipers had set their slippers. Each of the domes arching above the great room showed delicate stucco forms, almost as fine as the lace-like decoration of the Alhambra, vividly yet artistically coloured, with different quotations from the Koran at their base as a frieze. Filigree silver lamps hung from above, and a marble pulpit, reached by a long flight of steps, its rail also of marble, rose upon the side toward

Mecca; a less ornate but similar erection appeared on the opposite wall, whence an assistant reader had some part in Friday services.

The pleasant sound of running water, a distinctive feature of Mohammedan mosques, especially welcome in this dry and sun-baked land, filled the great edifice with a gentle murmur. A few devout Moslems entered, made their genuflexions and withdrew softly. Not essentially different, except in its numerous domes, from the ancient mosques in Algiers which are readily open to visitors, it was of greater interest in never having before admitted unbelievers, and there was no suggestion of " effect," with an eye toward tourist appreciation.

With an excess of courtesy, however, we were even permitted to ascend the slender green and white minaret, whence the hooded muezzin had made us familiar with his not always unmelodious intonation. The spiral stairway was decidedly contracted, and lined with reserve stores of small lamps full of oil;

so that during the climb I was forced to take my hat, almost my life, in my hand.

From the summit a vastly impressive view was gained, over the white city, the sapphire sea, and the yellow desert with its fringe of palms.

Interested spectators emerged upon surrounding roof-terraces, gazing upward at the unwonted sight of infidels ensconced on the very apex of holiness; but all seemed sufficiently friendly, and no suggestion that we should descend was made until the time approached for prayer-call.

The great mosque was dusky with twilight as we passed through, a few of the faithful silently prostrate; the narrow streets outside filled with donkeys and goats, vendors, camels, and countless nationalities seemed a different world.

But this was not our only experience of closed and hitherto unprofaned sanctuaries. Five years later, by invitation of the Pasha, who sent as our guard several imposing officers with yards of sword, we visited others, and heretofore the most inviolate, of these imposing edifices, even to the top of another lofty minaret. Manifestly to the consternation and disapproval of the caretakers, we stepped inside, removed our shoes as one would ·in a Buddhist temple in Japan, and gazed about the lofty interior. A certain guardian of a mosque peacefully slumbering at his post was summarily aroused by one of our Turkish escort with several well-directed blows of the flat of his sword, not necessarily painful except to dignity, but extremely effective for bringing to a sudden end such inopportune naps.

One of the most noteworthy mosques is the Jamah Hamed Pasha, near the gate Fum el-Bab. Known as the "great Caramanli mosque," it has a fine octagonal minaret. Its splendid pillars are of marble, and the walls up to the Koran frieze are formed of tiles, in soft greens and yellows with a bit of blue. The ceilings are decorated with great dignity, and the stair rails of inlaid marble are very

Several imposing officers with yards of sword

heavy and of good design. On each side of the arched alcove beside the pulpit, where the Imam prays when the muezzin above is calling to devotion, are huge brass candelsticks; beyond, a tall clock. Praying into this niche, the Imam will always face Mecca.

A small railed enclosure in one corner covered with a rug served some teacher as expounding ground to a class of young men, but it was primarily for the Friday seat of the Pasha. All the mosques had that feature.

The Sidi Dragut is said to contain relics of the prophet. The handsomest minaret, octagonal and lofty, with two balconies, adorns the mosque we had already visited, El-haj Mustafa Gurgeh of the seventeen domes, standing near the British Consulate. A pretty rounded minaret, also close by, was that of the mosque Jamah of Sidi Salem. All have fine and impressive features, and, the Pasha's will being law, we went to six or seven. In one was a carved screen to shelter the few women allowed to attend as a modern concession. The Mohammedans were most sincere in their religious convictions and practice, old Mufta of the Consulate being an especially handsome and noble specimen of the high-minded and religious Arab.

It is believed by experts in the history of religions that the Arabs are of Semitic stock, idolatry having been, about the time of Mohammed, but recently introduced among them. Even before the prophet certain reformers had similar ideals, of whom four of these thoughtful men were contemporaneous. While a most remarkable leader, the character and career of Mohammed were not beyond explanation. Men of the Jewish race were all about, and obligation to them was constant. He saw the advantage of having a sacred book, and sought to make alliance with them, but was not willing to take their book as the basis of a new religion. Yet borrowing continually from them for the Koran, especially from the Midrash of the Talmud, his perfected scheme shows also the influence of Zoroastrianism. He perhaps

MOSQUES

felt it necessary to make concessions to existing idolatry, as shown in the black stone of the Kaba at Mecca. Mohammed was undoubtedly sincere in the main, as are his followers to-day. And the constant turning toward Mecca, the utter devotion of the sober faces, became very impressive, as, all occupations instantly dropped for the moment, the mind was directed from this world to another.

XXV

Funerals

Frequently funeral processions swept through the streets, swiftly, silently. Over thirty men wrapped in white passed, one burning afternoon, chanting over and over again, very slowly and solemnly:

Two of them carried a coffin raised upon their heads, draped in rich and beautiful brightly striped silk, upon which lay two or three sleeveless jackets of velvet embroidered in gold. Just behind them followed a man bearing upon his head a tiny coffin covered with silk. Still behind walked three Moslem women, tightly wrapped in barracans, each with one dark eye uncovered, not quite so

162

Two domes on the headland, conspicuous as the harbour is entered

bright as usual. The strange, slow chant and swift procession were curiously affecting.

Two domes on the headland, conspicuous as the harbour is entered, were long supposed to be tombs of the Caramanli Pashas, but later researches have shown that a certain Sultana, misbehaving in Constantinople, was banished to Tripoli. So homesick as to become really ill, she begged that, dying on that far shore, she might be laid on land projecting as far as possible toward her beloved Constantinople. This accounts for one tomb; the other is probably that of a Caramanli Pasha.

Very beautiful must have been these graceful and richly decorated domes. Their ceilings still show a delicate tracery of Moorish stucco, originally lace-like and lovely. The fine green tiles, carved stone sarcophagi with tiled bases and exquisite finish throughout are now but wrecks of former beauty. Vandal hands have broken, stolen, mutilated, until only suggestions remain. Barbarous hordes have removed doors and everything else possible, have broken the

windows and reduced stone and tiles to fragments. Nature's elements have completed the
devastation.

Near by the Arab cemetery occupies a fine
promontory washed by gentle Mediterranean
surf.

A little farther away lies the English cemetery at Shara Shat, near which was the villa of
one of our English friends. Across the bay
and along a dazzling beach gleamed the
Pasha's castle. Hard it is to imagine that
ancient pile as turned to modern uses.

On one well-remembered afternoon the
domes and minarets of Tripoli stood out
against the sunset like some fairy city of a
dream. In imagination I had been trying
to reconstruct the daintiness of the original
decoration under the Caramanli dome, and to
follow backward the long, long story into a
vanishing past.

A grave had just been dug, for some old
woman, after the usual fashion not more than
eighteen inches deep. A few minutes later the

In the garden, Shara Shat

On the gallery

funeral train appeared. A richly dressed blind man led the small procession of white-draped men and women along the sandy way, two of the company bearing the coffin aloft as usual, and singing all together, this time very rapidly and constantly reiterated.

They stopped for five minutes in an angle of some buildings, while passages from the Koran were read; and everybody, instead of uncovering heads in respect, shielded them more completely, but removed their slippers. At the shallow grave the poor woman was taken from her coffin, merely a temporary receptacle, wrapped more tightly in her barracan, and placed in the grave, then covered thinly with earth and stones. A plaster slab would afterward be manufactured above her. So far, rich and poor were served alike; but the final form of the monument indicated the social status of the sleeper beneath. A pointed or gabled shape revealed his former humble station; a rectangular block with bowls or saucers sunken in the cement told a story of wealth and importance. These receptacles, however, were not for flowers, as one might imagine, but to hold water for birds. Every flat-topped grave had these merciful inserts. The birds are said to bring good fortune, so their drinking basins were not provided for wholly philanthropic reasons.

XXVI

AN ARAB LUNCHEON

"It is too hot to ride," said our interpreter on the day when we had been invited to an Arab luncheon given by one of the wealthiest Jewish families in Tripoli, at their country place about a mile down the beach.

Surrounded by gardens luxuriantly filled with flowers, fruits and vegetables, the great well constantly pouring into a large open cistern like a pleasure pond, from the center of which an ample fountain sprung upward all day long, this villa was one of the great estates of the region. But the *gibleh* had been blowing for two days, the air was scorching as a furnace, and a dim haze of desert dust filled every crevice. Even one's tightly shut watch and camera became impregnated with impalpable particles. The thermometer was

167

well above a hundred, but with air so dry it was no more uncomfortable than far lower temperatures nearer the equator, in jungle regions.

A narrow strip of shade lay along open streets close to the houses. Even the dusky Sudanese were lying in its welcome shelter, and not even a dog or a donkey ventured into the scorching glare.

"Too hot to ride!" I exclaimed, "I should think it much too hot to walk!"

"No," he replied. "Take umbrellas, go slowly — you will feel the heat less."

Knowing from long experience that native methods of combating or aiding climates are invariably best, I submitted, and we set forth, the only living beings astir.

Slowly following the narrow lines of shade, we soon emerged into the pitiless sunshine which seemed to grip one with scorching fingers. That mile was long to be remembered, but it came to an end at last, in gardens facing the sea.

168

AN ARAB LUNCHEON

When the servants had opened the great gates and ushered us in through the house doors, it was like entering a cellar. The dusky coolness seemed a haven of rest inside those thick walls where no heat could penetrate.

Iced drinks in tall glasses were brought at once, and my hostess soon appeared, very gorgeously arrayed in elegant native costume. This was full trousers of blue and white silk, barracan of pink silk, and sleeveless jacket of purple velvet heavily embroidered with gold. Her braided hair was tied into a blue and white silk handkerchief. Heavy earrings of unalloyed yellow gold weighted her ears and strings of sequins draped neck and shoulders. Wide bracelets, also of soft, pure gold, covered her arms nearly to the elbow, and her heelless gilt slippers were merely caught on her dainty toes. My prettiest embroidered white frock, which I had worn to honour the occasion, paled into utmost insignificance beside this array of splendour, and both my hos-

pitable hostess and several of her assembled
friends seemed to agree in that opinion.
Through the interpreter they asked many
questions about my garb — why I wore only
two colours, were n't the white shoes very hot,
and the gloves? Did I make the little embroidered flowers? They could appreciate that
work, but otherwise they evidently disapproved
politely of white gowns; and soon, surrounding me in a buzzing circle of interested and
rainbow-coloured femininity, they first inti-
mated gently and then definitely proposed that
I should be arrayed in garments similar to their
own. Like happy children, they followed me
to the large, airy bedroom of our hostess, stay-
ing until a set of wonderful articles was
chosen; and then courteously retired, leaving
two maids to help me into the unaccustomed
regalia.

I was fearfully and wonderfully composed!
The garments, in shape and texture like those
worn by all the other ladies, and of just as
many colours, were only slightly different in

combination; and except in the matter of hair-
dressing were quite becoming! The bracelets,
flat pieces of pure hammered gold, bent to fit
the arm, were so heavy and impervious that
they seemed the hottest things I had ever ex-
perienced. However, I was very proud of my
yards of precious sequins, and felt unusually
wealthy and important. When I emerged into
the drawing-room, there was a distinct sensation — enthusiasm knew no bounds. But more
than once before I was released, I sighed for
my cool white frock.

A stereoscope was produced, and all of us,
humble little oriental ladies, looked meekly at
the pictures, our only diversion.

As the household was not of the religion of
the prophet, the husbands of this company had
also been invited; soon they appeared, greeting us as we sat in a modest circle on the floor.
Among them came the Astronomer, evidently
much impressed by this array of splendour, and
quite failing to notice any previous acquaintance, so disguised by unaccustomed glory. I

heard him ask if I had not yet arrived — and at the moment happened to meet his eye. A more astonished scientist has rarely been seen. His expression was untranslatable; but with good grace he instantly accepted the situation, to the infinite delight of the ladies, who had gleefully watched his unconscious entrance.

Before long the company was summoned to the dining-room, cool, dim, with lofty ceiling, and many servants in waiting. Before each guest was a pile of ten or eleven plates, and the first course, placed upon the top one, was not wholly easy to manipulate. With its removal came a slight increase of comfort, which continued in arithmetical progression as the luncheon went on. Many delicious but mystifying Arab dishes were served, as well as the inevitable and always appetizing *cus-cus*, a variety of novel vegetables in hot and spicy sauces, and finally little cakes and welcome Turkish coffee.

It was after four o'clock before we rose from

A homeward ambling camel

AN ARAB LUNCHEON

the table, and nearly six when, once more arrayed in normal costume, I mounted a homeward-ambling camel, for a more familiar but equally delicious eight o'clock dinner at the Consulate.

XXVII

Eclipse Preparations

Selection of the exact spot for setting up
telescopes, finding workmen intelligent enough
for labours often exacting, a judicious choosing
among amateurs always more than ready to
" help," night-time testing of instruments for
weeks beforehand, engaging photographers
and fitting up temporary dark-rooms — all this
work the Astronomer must accomplish.

As far as mechanical preparation was concerned, we were hampered by the nationalities
and religions of the workmen, so that one set
or another was always off for its weekly holiday. No Mohammedan would work on Friday,
no Jew on Saturday, and Sunday was not on
our own list of toiling days. These three, with
the various feast and fast and sacred days of
the month Ramadan, interfered with astro-

Eclipse preparations

A spectral array . . . set to catch a shadow

nomical progress somewhat seriously. Also
the variation in language was often a barrier
to complete understanding of delicate points.
A few words of Arabic, Turkish, Greek and
Italian usually sufficed to get the day intelligently started, and the Astronomer's linguistic
facility soon placed his tasks well in hand by
the polyglot community. There was, too, one
never-failing resource, for when no Mediterranean tongue succeeded in impressing his
varied servitors, as a last resort he would hurl
a few emphatic Japanese words among his
waiting artisans, who, singularly enough, never
seemed to fail of his meaning when this acute
stage was reached.

In 1900 many telescopes were set up on the
Consulate terrace, all painted white, as well as
mountings and accessories, that they might
absorb less of the blinding heat in which all
day they baked — a spectral array, indeed, set
to catch a shadow. All were attached to one
large central tube, and each was furnished
with an endless chain of photographic plates

for exposure, making over a hundred pictures during the fifty seconds of totality.

The general idea was much the same as that of the Astronomer's former inventions used in Africa and Japan, in which pneumatic and electric power had each been successfully applied; but the depth of the Consulate courtyard made possible the use of mere gravity as the moving force, and an ingenious system of cords and pulleys was accurately adjusted. The cords were "tripped" at the proper point for exposures by beads from Moslem rosaries; the weights were buckets of desert sand.

A different but equally effective arrangement for the telescopes on the Consulate terrace was made for the second eclipse.

Certain reasons make it highly desirable to multiply photographs of the corona during a single eclipse. Many must still be studied before coronal nature can be fully known, its problems entirely unravelled. When that comes, the whole story of the sun can perhaps be told. Meantime, not only is it well to compare representations of many coronas of different years, which vary greatly in shape and size and evidences of solar activity, but to collate all those photographs taken during the swift progress of any one totality. Thus far no change in this delicate halo of ethereal light has been detected during its few moments of visibility at any given locality, nor even between the observable beginning and the end of the track, separated by more than two hours of actual time.

How rapidly, then, do alterations in the corona take place which, from one eclipse to another, modify its whole appearance — once a smooth circle, again a broken and irregular ring; sometimes showing long and immensely extended streamers, at the next occasion a quiet, petal-like development, without emphasis in any direction? No one has yet discovered.

A connection between sun-spot epochs and coronal streamers has been found. Sometimes, as we know, rapid changes occur in the spots, and probably the corona, invisible, may undergo similar fluctuations. If a hundred photographs of a single totality could be taken, extending from its first to its last second, not impossibly changes might be detected, undoubtedly faint and slight, but no less significant, beginning the riddle's answer. But the one, two or three minutes of most totalities are not enough for a single astronomer to take even twenty or thirty photographs by hand. Some mechanical means must be used to multiply them. And such a plan was again successfully carried out through the mechanical ingenuity of the Astronomer.

But even after all contingencies have been provided for, smaller necessities sometimes arise which could not have been anticipated. For instance, one day a few yards of catgut, or the strongest possible tennis-racquet or violin string was suddenly required. Never can I forget my frantic rush for catgut — wanted immediately. How to accomplish that strange errand in Arabic, I did not know. At so early a morning hour the special interpreter was not yet at hand, nor could our friends be found then at a moment's notice; but one of the clerks in the cable office who spoke a few words of English essayed to accompany me on this singular search.

At last he seemed to understand what was wanted, and away we sped. Ordinarily a very rapid walker, I soon found myself quite distanced. Without running, my guide made record time. From one place to another we went like the wind — but never found the catgut. The baggy Turkish trousers flew on ahead, and once the eager boy met an intimate friend, who evidently did not see me bringing up the rear. He came affectionately up to my courier, both hands outstretched in greeting. But my lad was not to be deterred from his quest. He took the friendly hands, indeed, but only for the purpose of putting their owner on one side, gently though with vigour. I still have the picture of that friend's grieved and amazed expression as he was thus summarily

179

dismissed, without an explanatory word, while his acquaintance sped on like fate, followed by a flying female in white.

One of the most interested spectators of the preparations was a deaf white Angora cat, which insisted upon examining every operation with much thoroughness. The Astronomer, being fond of these not ungentle adjuncts of humanity, was rather pleased at the constant attentions of his little friend, although she generally stationed herself for a comfortable nap in the tube of the telescope being at the moment adjusted. But one morning several things went wrong, and the calm philosophy to which I had grown accustomed was evidently broken, for bits of sentences emerged from the depths of instruments in which the astronomical head and person were immersed, suggestive of an almost mundane irritation. They gave me much glee, and were evidently uttered without thought of any possible auditor, sympathetic or foreign.

"One man Arabic, one Turk, one Maltese

ECLIPSE PREPARATIONS

— can't understand each other or me. Can't set down a cup of sand but some nationality steps into it. The deaf cat plays with pulleys and cords, until they are all tied up in knots, and might lead to Arcturus or Hades for all I can see. Where is my ——?" The rest became inaudible, trailing off into silence more significant than words.

But still the work progressed, whether the *gibleh* blew, bringing a fine golden haze of sand from the desert, turning the air hot and dry like a furnace, or whether the sea wind came in from the blue Mediterranean, making long and lovely days of fresh beauty to rival the rarest of remembered Junes.

And at last all was in readiness; it remained only for sun and moon and atmosphere to do their part.

XXVIII

THE ECLIPSE OF 1905

On this second visit more or less confidence was expressed that no harm would follow the eclipse, one old Arab remarking happily that the Astronomer came before to take their sun away, now he was coming to put it back, an operation of which he seemed distinctly to approve.

But belief was evident that hereafter such an occurrence was to be regularly expected every five years. I hope our numerous friends of many undistinguishable nationalities have not thought the war a result of our innocent eclipses; but they will have a long immunity. Although the sun may rise in eclipse in 1936, no corona will be seen again in Tripoli until 2027.

August 30 was coming on apace, and the day

Etim Bey, a Turkish exile

before grew very hot. For a week the Astronomer had not attempted to go to bed at all, catching a nap here and there as he could in intervals of observing stars, adjusting instruments and preparing generally; and one hour, or two at most, covered all the sleep he had in each twenty-four.

On eclipse day I rose as usual about four — so did the baker's smudge; but the Pasha had given orders, and no fires were made later in the day, the streets were sprinkled continually, to prevent possible dust, and the Franciscan Fathers had politely offered to have their church clock stopped from its loud striking during the eclipse, that those fleeting moments marked by Lieutenant Janoupoulus on our old Arab bell might not be interrupted by alien sounds.

The early morning sky was pale daffodil, with Orion and Sirius, Jupiter and Venus, shining resplendent; but the heat even then was remarkable in that land of life-giving breezes. A slight prophetic *gibleh* had begun the day before, which we hoped might be only a false alarm. But evidently there was reality in its warning, for the heat increased intolerably. By the time I reached the Consulate roof-terrace, where all was in readiness, the thermometer stood at a hundred and one. A fairly strong south wind blew, and all the time the sea horizon seemed drawing in, nearer and nearer, dim and beautiful, pale, smooth.

Beyond the Sultana's tomb the fringe of palms grew mistily yellow, the desert shimmered with heat. All the flags blew off toward the north, and Arabs, Jews, Italians, Maltese, even the Sudanese and Fezzani clung to the narrow shade strip in the street cañons far below. Sand suspended in the atmosphere was rising slowly from the horizon and staining the pure blue in an ever-ascending cloud. By ten o'clock it had risen three or four degrees. Overhead the sky was splendidly clear, deep blue, and unflecked by vapour. Above the Consulate courtyard it was like a square of dazzling sapphire.

THE ECLIPSE OF 1905

The Astronomer kept calmly on with his final preparations, not even glancing out to see how his sky was progressing, but I remember a distracted morning as I helped a bit here and there, then ran from balcony to terrace, from one corner to another to watch the advancing *gibleh* and its effect on the atmosphere. Steadily, but very deliberately rising, the yellow mass crept up the clear blue dome, ever reaching onward to the sun himself.

Dignified, handsome Challum, an Arab Jew, and head carpenter, had picked up half a dozen English words which he now brought forth reassuringly. " No *gibleh*, afternoon," he said, as I peered once more over the desert, thick, yellow, constantly nearer. An hour or so later he beckoned me to a far corner of the terrace, pointing seaward to a well-known reef.

" Look! " he said. One small whitecap broke lazily over the rocks out of a smooth and oily sea. This was his proof of change.

Before noon the hot blast ceased and windless silence fell. Every flag hung limp upon its mast. Then feebly, hesitatingly one or two stirred slightly, quivered, gave a fitful puff outward, and — away from the north! The sea wind was beginning — we were saved. Shortly after, they all stood out straight away from the blue Mediterranean, once more dark indigo and ruffled into a thousand joyous wrinkles and whitecaps. Within an hour the aspiring sand dropped back into its desert hills and valleys, once more the splendid air was free from stain, the horizon retreated, and clear and clean the afternoon drew on.

Gibleh was conquered.

Before first contact the usual rehearsal was conducted, with every one in his place, regular assistants and amateur helpers all in the blinding glare.

News of the eclipse was very general. In the open *suk*, or market, groups of men were sitting beside their camels in grave and serious, somewhat doubtful, expectation as the partial eclipse proceeded. At the open-air

cafès men would speak quietly of its progress, their companions answering, " May God
be gracious," when all lapsed into silence and
a certain awe.

Gradually, surrounding roofs filled. A few
wise persons had provided tent-like shelters
from the brightness, and all were supplied with
smoked glass. Instead of gazing steadfastly
at us, as the whole population had tried to do
in 1900, watching for some entertainment to
take place on the Consulate terrace, this time
all were looking at the sun.

First contact came promptly at 1.43. Very
quickly the bite out of the dazzling disc grew
larger, and the stout crescentic sun dwindled
rapidly. As before, the brilliant luminary was
more than half covered before any obvious
change occurred in light and heat. Everything
quieted so gradually that I was startled to
realize how the shadow had crept onward.
Materials for my drawing of the corona were
at hand, but they could not be used until
totality.

TRIPOLI THE MYSTERIOUS

The fine Gurgeh minaret with its two balconies towering above the mosque was filled with white-robed Moslems gazing skyward. As the light failed and grew lifeless and all the visible world seemed drifting into the deathly trance which eclipses always produce, an old muezzin emerged from the topmost vantage point of the minaret, calling, calling the faithful to remember Allah and faint not. Without cessation, for over fifteen minutes he continued his exhortation, in a voice to match the engulfing somberness, weird, insistent, breathless, expectant.

Between eight and ten minutes before totality a strange appearance began to sweep across the whiteness of the terrace at my feet. For an instant I failed to recognize what I had always looked for in previous eclipses, and had never seen, but which nevertheless I was even at that moment expecting.

As I saw the strange wavering light and darkness, my first thought was, " Why! the *gibleh* stopped! There are no clouds! What

188

The fine Gurgeh minaret . . . was filled with white-robed Moslems
gazing skyward

is coming between us and the last remnants of sunlight? "

For one brief instant I thought of drifting smoke. Then with a start I realized that at last I was seeing actual " shadow bands " — that strange quiver of mystery which creeps or rushes or glides across the world just before the moon's shadow completely envelops the landscape. It affected me singularly, and I observed the bands with great care. Both the lines of light and shadow were very narrow, not much over an inch in width, not straight, but slightly and irregularly curved. As I faced the sun, my back about northeast, the lengthwise stretch of the bands was from me toward the sun, and they moved eastward with great rapidity, thus at right angles to their own direction as well as to that of the wind, though not absolutely straight — rather a huge curve or part of a circle whose center was the sun.

Elusive as wraiths they drifted past me, along our own terrace, the lower roofs and

off over the city. I should not say they rushed
along, though the speed was very great; the
motion was infinitely more airy and exquisite
and fitful than any one word could convey. A
pedestrian could not have kept pace with them.
Rising and falling in intensity, they faded, almost fainted, from sight, and five times they
rose again, clear and distinct. Absorbing as
this strange appearance was, I nevertheless
had to watch for totality, to give the signal
for Lieutenant Janoupoulus to announce on
the old Arab bell. Also, I was to look for the
final breaking up of the slender crescent into
Baily's Beads, so marked a phenomenon of the
1900 eclipse. But they did not appear this
time.

The crescent melted from sight — the last
ray of true sunlight was quenched, and for
twenty seconds I had seen the corona nearly
complete to the failing bright spot. It seemed
so struggling to emerge, to come into sight
and knowledge of men, that it *must* show itself
even before the appointed time.

THE ECLIPSE OF 1905

The moment of totality produced an immense impression all over the city. Those detailed to watch its effect upon the inhabitants reported that nearly all stood up, while ejaculation and prayer arose from hundreds, even thousands of voices. Many spread their hands to heaven toward the sun, saying, " God is great," " What God willed came to pass," " May God be gracious to His servants."

When first the corona flashed unmistakably into the deep blue sky, the entire city burst into irrepressible applause, a rolling wave of sound that spread and spread from sea to silent desert and out into immensity.

Freighted with some new message from the sun, mysterious, always invisible except during these flying moments, the corona knows its own pale beauty and import, and would reveal its secret if permitted. Once again in the limpid African firmament it bloomed, even as the celestial flower whose perfectness had haunted me for five years, its petals white with the vivid fire of æons and the struggle of un-

191

imaginable conflagrations, its center the dark
moon ball hung there by mighty force to show
this pregnant blossoming, then carried on and
away relentlessly. But the flower is always
there, only our clumsy means have not yet revealed the waiting secrets.

Evenly developed all around, another proof
of the suspected connection between the corona
and sun-spot periods, there were many bright
streamers, but no long ones. Considerable
detail of interwoven filaments was evident, but
this was not a spectacular corona; it was a
halo, round, yet sharply pointed. I drew, and
drew, and looked and drew again; and all the
time the inexorable bell struck out its warning
every fifteen seconds. One of the least dark
of total eclipses, all sketching went on merely
by coronal light. For three minutes and over
the wondrous spectacle lasted. All the lower
sky was warm yellow, and Venus sprang out
as newly made, from sky depths instead of
sea. The Tarhuna mountains leaped into
singular, sudden purple prominence.

Evenly developed all around

THE ECLIPSE OF 1905

An intense silence fell over city and gardens, while the rare heaven flower bloomed. And then — a gleam of actual startling sunlight shot down, but I was able to follow the corona for many seconds after. It seemed to fade reluctantly, as if loath to leave hurrying cameras, eager telescopes, hastening pencils. But common life and daylight returned, as they always seem to do after these moments of uplifted silence.

With a few noteworthy exceptions, eclipses rarely bring discoveries of a sensational nature. Expeditions generally return bringing just a little more light on some large solar problem, the whole to be solved only after repeated attacks during the eagerly seized moments of many eclipses. This one proved conclusively the law, now fully established, that the 1905 type of corona is inseparably related to a thickly spotted sun. But why? The answer must come through some new magnetic theory of the distribution of the sun's radiant energy.

TRIPOLI THE MYSTERIOUS

To a truly scientific mind even a fraction of actual fact, newly learned, is to be cherished, debated; and if countless expeditions should be required to complete the whole, astronomers would still feel amply repaid for any exertion.

What is so valuable as truth? And truth is fact, often painfully dug out through years of toil and devotion.

The astronomer deals in cycles, and rarely expresses his periods in terms of years. As the practically inconceivable distance of sun from earth is the footrule of the universe, so the measure of astronomic time is groups of centuries; persistent patience the astronomer's first characteristic.

Perfectly the apparatus had worked, long days and nights of sleepless devotion were rewarded.

The dark-room was full of records; the eclipse was over.

XXIX

The Desert

In seashore towns one feels the ocean calling. Always there is the undercurrent of knowing it is there. One may not recognize its compelling presence — traffic, talk, teas, barter and gain may go on with apparent unconsciousness; but that great proximity is never quite absent from the constant life of the community.

In Tripoli one similarly feels the rolling Sahara — it is there, close-creeping, brooding, waiting — with an awfulness not to be explained, an immensity like the ocean itself, a fascination almost uncanny in its wind-swept spaces.

Narrow lanes ankle deep in sand between mud walls and thickets of olives came suddenly to an end, and before us was eternity in

195

visible form. No matter how hot the city, over the sand a fresher air seemed always to prevail, an etherealization of breathing, perfection of experience possible to the lungs. Who minded a world enwrapped in blinding sunshine, or the blue fire of the heavens, when air fit for the gods, the very elysium of ether, was filling one with a strange ecstasy of life!

The oasis was left behind. Here a few castor-oil plants, there a milkweed or two, sparse grass, last outpost of vegetation creeping away in clumps, all soon ceased, and only the high sand ridges, a yellow spray whirling off the sharp-edged tops like snowdrifts, the wind, sunset and silence remained— a blessed healing silence, and air like wine. As far out as the eye could reach, the horizon blended in soft, bluish tints, atmospheric and lovely.

A string of camels moved off across the illimitable sand, a marabout dome rose whitely, and a shepherd in gracefully looped brown barracan, conducting his flock of goats, played on the strange bagpipes with an effect of unmiti-

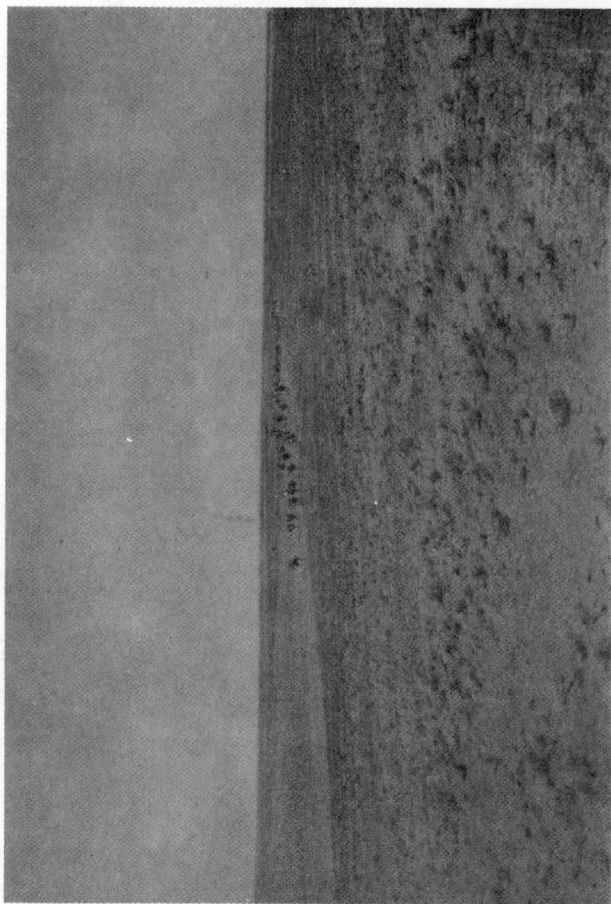

A string of camels moved off across the illimitable sand

gated barbarism. Behind him as he strode
along rose the pillars of the last well, and a
few camels were already lying down for the
night under its scattered palms. One tree more
venturesome than the rest grew far out beyond
the others, and as evening approached a lithe
Arab walked boldly up its stem to fasten at the
top his earthen " monkey " for the night's drip
of *lakbe*. In the morning a mild beverage,
only pleasantly intoxicating, would fill the receptacle. If put up early in the day and left
until evening, a more fiery liquid is thought
to be collected.

Could one ever become familiar with that
enormous waste of splendour and glory, of
richness and desolation! Grand in its cruelty,
pitiless in beauty, it fascinates, appalls, enchains
without trying, superbly indifferent whether or
not we care, enriching or annihilating with
equal aloofness, radiant in atmosphere, awful
in extent, impermanent yet eternal.

Silent as the great sky spaces, wind-swept
like the hills of God, waiting passionless for

some enormous revelation still to come, Sahara
bides his time. And men and camels go and
come in pitiful little companies, their tracks of
to-day obliterated to-morrow, traversing bits
of the immensity, suffering fatigue, thirst, heat-
strokes as they go, yet the calm desert broods
on uncaring, itself part of that eternity which
cannot ever be conquered or understood or
companioned, constantly changing, yet always
and forever the same.

Here and there high, soft hills gave vantage
for viewing the uneven waste, rippled by the
wind into a million lovely waves, rhythmic,
regular. Ridges and mounds apparently permanent are really as evanescent as the scenery
of a dream. The gentle summer breeze blowing with such dry, enchanting softness is the
iron hand in the velvet glove, as irresistible
as doom, carving hills and valleys to suit itself,
lifting the entire desert surface off and on at
its own wild will. Restless, changeful, uneasy,
it makes and unmakes capricious scenery.
Over the treeless waste a camel here and there

198

A well of sweet water on the edge of the desert

or a nomadic Bedouin encampment was sole evidence of human life. Even the ridge on which I stood might be gone to-morrow, a hollow in its place.

Silence that could be felt, dryness that singed yet exhilarated, loneliness beyond words, and soothing stretches of warmly undulating palpitating yellow sand flowed about one's consciousness like an unfathomable sea.

A Buddha for calm irresponsiveness, Nirvana in its power to bring forgetfulness, a Sphinx for mystery profound and impenetrable, eternity in its silent promise and trembling hope, the desert seems not bounded by terrestrial limits. It is a psychical condition, outside and beyond geographical terms. Nothing nearer than the aurora borealis could touch it on the north, or than the southern cross on its far spaces in great African wilds. Sunrise and sunset are its only limits. Time here joins hands with infinity, with the very gods who stay no more on earth, but now and then vouchsafe a glimpse of their wonder and

endlessness. The soul might even find itself
in desert spaces, where the voice of God is
audible, and the breath of man annihilated.

As the mysterious wind increased, pure beyond all humanity's needs, eddies and currents
and drifts of sand began to hurry and cascade
and circulate, like light snow in a New England
winter, until a golden haze crowned every hill,
and tumbled off in waves of glory from every
ridge.

The sunset glowed and burned, intensified
into concentrated colour and majesty, and one
or two date palms stood out in silhouette
against its celestial conflagration. The surface
of the sand cools as evening comes on, but
underneath it is still hot with remembrance of
noon.

Silent, soft-footed camels passed like shadows of grotesque thoughts in the gathering
dusk, and the stars burned singularly near
and brilliant in the velvet blue sky. Never,
even at sea, do stars seem so close, so gorgeous, yet so friendly as over the illimitable

The sunset glowed and burned

wastes of the warmly pulsing desert, through its dry and fragrant air, when the happy wind has softened to a sweet breathing.

Over the sand, out of the sunset, filling the sky, voices whispered which speak only here, and strange currents from some life other than this flowed through and onward like an immortal atmosphere. The sand gleamed white and spectral through miles of distance, the stars drew nearer and more near, and desert murmurs clung to innermost consciousness, while life held its breath almost for pain, yet with inexplicable joy, waiting for — who could say what divine afflatus!

XXX

B' SALAAMA

The fascination of life in a region so composite grew with each day. Square houses like solid blocks of white masonry, domed mosques and tombs; upward-springing minarets crowned by golden star and crescent; fine Moorish tiles brutally whitewashed; the pathetic memorials of Rome's greatness, the halted arts and industries — all combined to give full sway to amazement, deepest interest, regret, unavailing desires.

Can one properly call this heterogeneous mass of humanity a people? Are their rude leather cushions, straw dish-covers, rugs, imperfect carving and metal working, weaving and pottery art at all? And was it the iron hand of Mohammedanism, the deadening

202

Upward-springing minarets

power of Turkish rule, or the inertia of the desert which was to blame for this sleeping province?

Whatever it may have been, Tripoli was a city of enchantment, white as dreams of Paradise, fringed by palms and olives, and steeped in memories of the centuries.

Near the recently completed Roman Catholic church, attended chiefly by Italians and Maltese, were a monastery on whose roof-terrace the brown-robed, rope-girdled friars walked at sundown, and a convent, whose sweet-faced Sisters asked us if Spanish was the only language spoken in America. From high minarets the resonant call of the muezzins to prayer was interspersed with church bells, as artistically inconsistent with the scenes about as the penetrating notes of an untuned piano issuing from a certain pink dwelling in joyous rag-time performed by one deeply satisfied Maltese maiden. But these were foreign influences hardly affecting the oriental atmosphere. Luncheons in harems, weddings at which not even the bridegroom was present, afternoon coffee in gardens where the Turkish band discoursed interrogative music — the golden days slipped by like enchantment, and Tripoli crept close into our hearts, never to be indifferently remembered.

With unmounting and packing of telescopes, and general demolition of the " royal observatory," I found that the strange, sordid, poetic city had taken fast hold of my heart. Certain places, surroundings, persons, even casually seen, are instantly recognized as one's own. They belong vitally to ourselves. Tripoli and its desert were never alien, despite all the strangeness of first impressions.

There was no brass plate to step on, no seagate to pass through in 1905, so there is no oracular certainty that we shall ever return. But I feel it notwithstanding. Once more I shall see that noble bay curving to meet its dazzling sands. Once more I shall breathe that extraordinary air, fresh from the laboratory of a new creation.

Once more I shall see that noble bay

B' SALAAMA

Everybody came to see us off; the old pier was crowded by friends and many followed us out to the *Djurjura*, on whose pleasant after-deck we had good-bye tea served just before sailing. Our special escort in the swift gig flying the English Consulate flag was the Consul, with splendid Mufta and Mohammed. Several Greek officers came off in their launch from the *Crete*, and the Pasha sent his fare-wells by officials of the Castle who brought presents and every good wish. Two of our most valued English friends were last to leave us. The final moments were non-hilarious.

The close-creeping desert with its exquis-itely pure air, the palms and gardens, the city itself — all came in one bewildering retrospect, as I watched the strip of blue water widen between our little steamer and all those enchantments.

The high white Consulate grew smaller with distance; the friendly British flag floated over a balcony full of friendly faces and hands waving farewell.

TRIPOLI THE MYSTERIOUS

And now Tripoli has been bombarded — her conquerors changed once more, in the long story of her vicissitudes. That old lighthouse is a shapeless white mass; and all the sleepy life is shaken from its lethargy. The fertile soil, always lurking beneath encroaching sands, waiting only for water to burst into blossom and fruit, will be cultivated and encouraged. The creaking wells, unchanged since the days of Carthage, will soon give way to modern reservoirs, pipes will replace goatskins, machinery will take the work of patiently pacing cows as motive power. After its newest crisis the city will progress in modern ways; there may even be telephones, electric light, paving, automobiles — sometime.

But the desert cannot be conquered at once, nor the Tuaregs who traverse its mysterious spaces. Always there will be strange miles of golden sand where lurks infinity.

All uncleanness seems washed clean in its lonely stretches; the life-giving sun and ardent air must still bring singular joy, the eager morning breeze, the opalescent distance, the plaintive evening sky— all will continue to tell an exquisite if inarticulate story.

That Tripoli will remain, whatever the Powers may decree.

INDEX

INDEX

INDEX

211

INDEX

212

INDEX

213

INDEX